Always On the Move

Teens in Care Write About Changing Homes

By Youth Communication

Edited by Laura Longhine

I0156419

YOUTH COMMUNICATION

True Stories by Teens

Always On the Move

EXECUTIVE EDITORS
Keith Hefner and Laura Longhine

CONTRIBUTING EDITORS
Al Desetta, Nora McCarthy, Autumn Spanne, Jennifer Chauhan,
Kendra Hurley, and Philip Kay

LAYOUT & DESIGN
Efrain Reyes, Jr. and Jeff Faerber

COVER ART
Gabriel Sanchez

For reprint information, please contact Youth Communication.

ISBN 978-1-933939-89-6

Second, Expanded Edition

Printed in the United States of America

Youth Communication ®
New York, New York
www.youthcomm.org

Table of Contents

Contents

Contents

Contents

Introduction

One of the most painful parts of living in foster care is the lack of permanence. On top of leaving their homes and families, and not knowing when or if they'll be back, too many kids are moved from placement to placement once they're in foster care. Adding to the problem is an often heavy turnover among staff members and social workers. For teens who crave permanence and a sense of connection with others, all of this dislocation can be hard to handle.

In this book, teens in care discuss the impact of moving from home to home, and their struggles to keep in contact with the important people in their lives. They give specific advice to staff and foster parents on how to ease the pain of impermanence.

In "Too Many Schools," Akeema Lottman describes one of the biggest challenges facing teens who move around a lot—having to change schools. Akeema attends four different high schools in four years, and struggles to get teachers and administrators to accept her credits and pay attention to her needs. Still, she manages to graduate. She advises other teens to advocate for themselves and find an adult who can help them. In the story that follows, she interviews a legal expert for advice on the educational rights of youth in care.

Other stories describe additional losses teens experience when they move, including leaving behind caring foster parents, friends, and neighborhoods. Sometimes, those moves are worth it. In "Goodbye, Harlem," for example, Antwaun Garcia describes how going into foster care and moving to a safe neighborhood in Queens changed his life for the better.

But other times, moves are unnecessary and can be prevented by better communication between staff and teens. Charlene Johnson, for example, describes how she was removed from a loving foster home in order to be placed with biological siblings she wasn't close to.

"I think the child welfare workers thought they were doing a good thing by moving Charlotte and me back with our sisters," she writes. "But if they had actually taken the time to speak to us, they would have found out that we didn't want to move."

In many of the stories, teens stress the importance of finding a reasonably good match between teen and foster parent before the teen moves in, to minimize the likelihood that the placement won't work out and the teen will have to move again. And part of making placements work is training foster parents about what to expect.

Baudilio Lopez describes the troubling cycle that happens when agencies, eager to place their foster kids quickly, send them to foster parents who are uninformed and ill-prepared to deal with teens who may be mistrustful or traumatized. When kids act out, they are "returned," making it even harder to them to adjust to the next new home.

"They [foster parents] don't understand that we foster kids aren't apple trees that you can grow with cheap fertilizer and then live off of," he writes. "In fact, we're more like delicate and exotic plants that need all your time, attention, and skills."

It's not only foster parents who need to do the work—teens need to reach out, too. In their stories, twin sisters Aquellah and Taheerah Mahdi explain how bouncing in and out of bad foster homes has made it hard for them to give a new parent a chance. In "Take It Slow," a therapist offers advice on how to adjust to a new home, and when it's best to move on.

When teens and foster parents or staff are willing to meet each other halfway, they can overcome the instability of the past. In the last story in this book, Manny S. describes arriving at his third foster home, at age 8, with little expectation that he'd be staying long.

"I'd started to believe that all my experiences in foster care would be negative," he writes. "I was trapped in a circle of revolving doors, and I didn't think I'd ever be able to stay in one place."

But his third foster mother is caring and patient. She doesn't push him to open up, but she's consistent in her care. Gradually, they develop a bond. As Manny's story shows, when teens find homes where they're understood and feel safe (and are allowed to stay there), they can begin to trust enough to finally feel at home.

Baudilio Lozado

The Moving Game

By Quantwilla Johnson

If you've been in foster care more than a few months, you know a lot about "the moving game." That's when the foster care system moves you from place to place without telling you when or why it's happening. This causes a lot of pain for kids who've already suffered enough.

I was in and out of seven foster homes between the ages of 3 and 10. I never knew why I was moved, and I was always upset when I was placed in a new home. Why is a child suddenly told to pack her bags without an explanation? I was never told if I was being moved because of a decision by my agency, my social worker, or my foster parents.

I think kids have a right to know why they're being taken out of a home and placed somewhere else. Foster children should also have a say in where they're about to be placed.

It seemed like the good homes were the ones I was quickly taken from, while the homes where I was mistreated were the ones I stayed in the longest. I really don't think that they paid enough attention to me if they left me in the bad homes and took me out of the good ones.

hen I was placed in my first home I liked it a lot. I could feel the love when I stepped in the door, and I never felt like an outcast. The main reason I liked living there was that we did things as a family, like playing games, going out together, and spending quality time together.

I needed love because I was coming from a foster home where I had experienced physical, mental, and verbal abuse. I was hit with anything in sight, called names, and never shown any love. So when I came to the home of the foster mother I'll call Jane, it was paradise. I thought that this would be my home, and I wanted to stay there a long time.

I never knew why I was moved, and I was always upset when I was placed in a new home.

But the next thing I knew I was being snatched from Jane's home. After only about one month, I was suddenly told to pack my bags and be ready when my social worker came. I felt angry because I thought my social worker could have at least warned me. As a result, I raised hell when they tried to take me. I kicked and screamed and hid from my social worker.

Even though I was only 6, too young to completely understand why I was being taken away, I think I should have been told something.

After leaving Jane's house, I was placed in another good home, but I tried not to love my new family because I knew what was going to happen. Sure enough, before I could even tell my new foster family that I loved them, I was taken away again after only three months.

My last foster home is the one I've been in now for about

seven years. It took a while to get there, but I made it, and I love my family very much. I get everything I want and this home is permanent. The best feeling of all is that I know that I won't be taken away.

Now that I'm older, I would definitely ask why I was being moved if it ever happened again. I would want to know who made the decision, why I was being taken away, and if I could stay if I wanted to. No foster child should go through what I did.

Being moved caused me a lot of pain in the past and I still feel it now. I'll never forget the pain and horror of being pulled from a loving home.

Quantwilla was 17 when she wrote this story.
She later attended SUNY-Purchase, majoring in social work.

Rosa Perin

Gotta Leave Again

By Forever Broughton

I've been in foster care for 18 years and, at 19, I'm still in it. In all, I've been in five homes, and in many of those homes I felt like a stranger most of the time. I felt like I didn't know what to expect when I walked into a room. Then, every time I finally got comfortable in a placement, I was moved again.

Half of the homes I was in I didn't even get a chance to get comfortable.

Once, when I was 10, they moved me and my sister to a home that wasn't even ready for us. The first night in that new home, I slept in a bed that wouldn't be mine later on that night. When the bed's owner got home, I had to go and make myself a new bed. Other things weren't prepared: sheets weren't on the beds, the rooms were disorganized, and the closets were already full. I didn't expect it to be like that. I was expecting things to be organized so I could feel at home.

Weeks later, I still wasn't totally comfortable, but was starting to feel all right there. There was nothing to complain about and I was getting used to the home. But before I knew it, I was moved again. Why? I think it was because the social worker thought I should be living with relatives. I had never lived with anybody in my family before, but the next place I moved to was with my relatives. Maybe it was a good idea for the social workers to put me with family, but I wish they had thought of that in the first place. Then maybe I wouldn't have had to be moved so much.

I felt most comfortable in that next home. Part of it was because I was there for a long time. When you live somewhere for over a year, instead of just getting used to being with the family and adjusting to them and their neighborhood, you get to settle in. Also, when you don't move around you don't have to change schools. But the main reason why I was comfortable in that home was because if you are in a home for more then a year, you feel wanted there. So when I live in a home for a while, I know I'm with people who love me, care about me, and want me.

When you live somewhere for over a year, you get to settle in. You feel wanted there.

I lived in that house for eight years. Everything was around there. I had friends, the park, the store right around the corner. The train was near by, so were the buses. Besides, this was the family I grew to love.

I was 8 years old when I arrived there, and at first I felt like a stranger. I didn't know what to expect from the family or the house. I didn't know if it was going to be the same thing all over again.

But I got comfortable quickly because as soon as I walked into the home they introduced me to the video games. The family took care of the rest of the things, like my clothes—they hung them up and all that. They talked to me about washing the dishes and cooking so that when I grow up I won't have to depend on someone to cook or clean for me. The way they spoke to me made me feel it was important for me to be someone.

But after eight years there, the social workers came into the home when we didn't have any heat. It was winter. All families can't always pay their bills on time. Social workers should understand that. Instead, the social workers didn't listen. They did what they thought would be best for me, not what I knew was best.

It's just hard starting life all over, and feeling like a stranger all the time.

I thought it was best for me to stay in that house where I felt love. When the social worker asked if I was happy there and did I want to stay, I pleaded, "Yes," but the social worker found the family guilty of something so innocent, and I was moved. I felt heart-broken.

When my sister and I got to the next home the social worker put us in, we had to start all over again. That feeling was not good. The neighborhood had a lot of people on the corner looking like they were out for trouble. When I entered the home, I felt like a stranger all over again.

It's just hard starting life all over, and feeling like a stranger all the time. Making new friends ain't all pleasure, and neither is getting used to new surroundings. I don't think anyone wants to always be a stranger.

But that's how I've almost always felt, because the people who made the decisions for me didn't always make the right ones. What I'm saying is: They messed up my life. When they moved me out of that home, they took me away from the people I love. They broke up a happy family. They kept on moving me and that made me so confused. We moved too much and started over too many times. I moved so much that I didn't care where I ended up as long as my sister was with me. The only comfort of it all was that my little sister was always with me.

My sister's name is Shaquin, and she's 15. We've been together in every house. She has been through the same things I went through. The thing we talk about most is: Why do we keep moving from place to place?

Having my sister helps me let my feelings out. She can expose her feelings, so when she's around it's easier for me to do it, too. My sister lets me know it's all right because we're together. She makes me feel like she's the only thing I should live for. After our mother died it's been only me and her. So that's why I stick by my sister each moment I've been moved. I know my mother would want my sister with me.

Forever was 19 when he wrote this story.

Advice to Foster Parents and Social Workers

Because I've moved so much, I have some good ideas for how foster parents and social workers can help make a kid in their care feel more comfortable. Here are a few ways I thought of:

• **Foster kids should get a chance to meet the parents before entering the home.**

That way the child can say if she is going to feel happy with the parent she might spend the rest of her life with.

• **Please have beds and all rooms prepared for the child's arrival.**

In half of the homes I've been in these things were not in place, and it made me feel unwanted.

• **Have something fun to do.**

Playing video games helped me feel comfortable more quickly in the home I lived in for eight years.

• **Make sure the child has easy transportation to school.**

Either the foster parent must have a car to drive us to school or we should be living close to our school. Otherwise, if the child has to get up extra early for school, she's going to be too tired to go. That's why some kids fail school. It happened to me.

• **Be a good foster parent to a foster child.**

How? It's simple. Treat a foster child like she's your own. If you're not able to treat the child like that, don't even think about getting one.

• **Listen to the child and what she or he wants.**

The child is the best person to say whether a home is good or bad, so listen to the children. To my own social workers, I'd just like to say that when I'm happy in a home, please trust me and believe me and don't move me again, and I won't let you down.

—**Forever Broughton**

YC Art Dept.

Looking for One Good Home

By Hattie Rice

About six months ago my group home started to change more than Michael Jackson's face. And as with his face, it got worse.

First our supervisor bounced. Then one of our realest staff, Ms. Deidra, went into the lost and found. Then we lost our social worker, who I was just starting to open up to. That was like having the house's legs snatched out from under me.

We got mad cornballs coming to replace our good staff. That's how the wilding out began. About six months ago, everybody in the house just started bugging out.

Luckily I'd already spread the word that I wanted to be moved to a foster home, and the search was on. I imagined living with the perfect Brady Bunch family. (OK, maybe not that perfect but at least the Cosbys.)

I pictured a house in the suburbs, with a yard out back and a car out front. I wanted a family that could give me what my parents couldn't: stability. I wanted to feel safe and protected. Who could do that better than Mr. Brady and Marsha?

Then one day ACS (the city's foster care agency) came to the door and asked to talk to each of us separately. They told me that my house was closing. I was so happy! Hell, I'd been collecting bags just waiting for the day.

The only thing that scared me was the deadline. I mean, how do you plan on kicking 11 kids out of house and home within a month? Suddenly I felt scared about the home I might get put in. (Then again, could it drive me crazier than this place?)

After they announced the closing, I talked to my social worker about my concerns, but she seemed as clueless as the residents. Everybody had heard something different and the residents knew almost nothing.

I wanted a family that could give me what my parents couldn't: stability.

A couple of days after ACS came, the staff told us about a speakout to help recruit foster parents for teens. They asked the residents to each write a speech. In my speech, I said that some foster parents are looking for someone to mold, so they prefer babies, but that they should consider having foster teens in their homes. Foster teens are strong and unique, and they need a parent to guide and love them as much as any baby—even if they express their feelings with negativity sometimes.

I wrote in my speech, "Teens are rare jewels that have survived the trials and tribulations of foster care. The courage they exhibit is monumental and a strength that all can learn from. The most important quality teens have is their ability to love, unlike babies, who need to be loved and nurtured."

I wanted them to understand how much a good family could mean to each of us. At the end I wrote, "All we have ahead of us is a bunch of closed doors. If you open the door to your heart I'd gladly step in."

B ut at the speakout, I felt disappointed. I was looking for a home, but it looked like some of the foster parents needed the home more than me. I mean, it looked like a straight homeless shelter up in there: A guy in the tightest, 10-years-too-young-for-him sweats with a shirt neither a washing nor an ironing could fix. A lady who looked like something out of *Flashdance*, with puffy hair and a bright pink and white polka dot shirt.

One man seemed to be the average pervert who sits on the porch saying, "Damn," to all the pretty girls that pass. As soon as I walked in the room, his face just lit up. Then we had your project girl who had kids with her but looked no more than 22. I thought, "How do you plan on showing us right if you couldn't even manage to not get pregnant as a teen?"

Finally, there was a guy who, at one point in the meeting, got up and banged on the desk and just sat back down. Looking at that crowd, I was furious and scared. These people didn't look like the type of family that could help me do right.

When it came time to speak, I introduced myself, read my speech, and answered a few questions about myself. One person asked me to say some of my qualities. I told them, "I don't talk," which scared the living daylights out of them. Mission complete. I didn't want any of those people to be my foster parents. By that time, I figured ACS was full of horse Sugar Honey Iced Tea.

My group home was supposed to close by Aug 31. Then ACS said we've got until Nov 31. Now they say it's Oct. 31. I want to move out and move soon.

A couple weeks ago my worker called me and said we needed to go meet some lady in Brooklyn. On the way to her house, I was gassed as if I was going to see B.I.G. resurrected. Then we pulled up to this stuck-up little brick house with a jacked-up car to match. I knocked on the door and out came a shriveled-up, mean looking old lady. She was very outspoken. You could tell who wears the Tims in that family, and who be stomping who out.

The thing that stuck to me was when she asked, "Can I discipline you?" I know you're thinking, "In which way?" If you'd seen the evil gleam in her eyes you would be sure she meant in the physical way.

She also said she wants to give me a curfew. Well, her curfew—7 p.m.—might work for kids born in 1883. I'm sitting up there trying to explain to her that I ain't no Jack the Ripper on the loose.

I did not want to be living one-on-one with this lady. The only thing we could relate about is being female, black and alive. If that's the case, Whitney Houston might as well be my foster mom, long as Bobby don't touch me.

Even my social worker thought that lady was bugged. On the way home we talked and she said, "I don't even know why you were brought here. All they had to do was ask me and I could have told them it wouldn't work."

I was pissed because I believed ACS would find a good home for me. They seemed quick to forget what I said about preferring to live in the suburbs. The situation reminded me of living at home with my parents. The more I tell them what I want, the less they listen. It's my life, but it seems their main objective is to do what they want, no questions asked.

Since then, I haven't heard a thing. I'm suffering. I feel like a baby who's been neglected by her parents, ACS. It seems they forgot about Brown Sugar. I don't know how they could forget about all this sweetness, but maybe they have.

I feel lost, like I'm in the middle of the ocean with no Christopher Columbus to lead me to a New World. I can only hope my final destination will be the one ACS and I planned: a permanent home with a family that can help me leave my past behind.

Hattie was 15 when she wrote this story. She later graduated from high school and went to college.

Kevin Cobham

Mail-Order Children

By Baudilio Lozado

The life of a foster child (myself included) is similar to that of a wandering nomad: we're always moving to where the grass is supposedly greener, only to find that the land is barren and we must move on.

The difference is: the wandering nomad moves about freely, having only himself to blame for any misfortune he finds along the way. The foster child, by contrast, lives the life of a used product that is found "defective" by the foster family, "recycled" to the agency, and resold to the next sucker who comes along (trust me—I've been recycled among five foster homes).

The foster care experience is traumatic, any way you look at it. It is especially painful to be torn from your biological parents after the first few years of development, when you've come to accept them as the real deal. Because by that time you are able to determine that, invariably, "Mommy" is Mommy and "Daddy" is Daddy. Period. This is a bond that should never be broken. But when it is...well, you have a broken child. Yet many foster parents don't seem to realize that you can't simply "raise" a child who has gone through this experience.

They don't understand that we foster kids aren't apple trees that you can grow with cheap fertilizer and then live off of. In fact, we're more like delicate and exotic plants that need all your time, attention, and skills. Otherwise, we die.

> ***Foster kids aren't apple trees that you can grow with cheap fertilizer. We're more like delicate and exotic plants that need all your time, attention, and skills***

However, a lot of foster parents see their acceptance of a foster child as an act worthy of sainthood (well, Amen to you, pal), which should be rewarded in the form of unconditional love and appreciation from the child—not to mention monthly checks from ACS. Some even break up inside if their foster kids don't love them. (If you want unconditional love, get a pet.)

So when the foster kid (already frightened and confused from being kidnapped) fails to reward the foster parents with her quota of unconditional affection and gratitude, the foster home falls apart.

You see, if there is no unconditional love coming from the foster parents themselves, the happy medium between pampering a child and giving discipline is lost. I mean, if you're a foster parent who fits this description, what's stopping you from throwing the boy or girl who "acts up" out the window? You don't love them, they're not really yours. Right?

You want to know what eventually happens? Well...what would you do if you found that the perfect child you expected wasn't so perfect after all?

I don't know about you, but what many foster parents do when the product (us) doesn't live up to their expectations is (you guessed it) demand a refund.

This foster kid cycle can trace its origins to the very heart of the system. In their haste to find "suckers" to buy their "products," the agencies have resorted to lies and false advertising—which means false information about the child, or no information at all.

I remember the surprised looks on my new foster parents' faces when they saw how poorly clothed I came from my last foster home. Or their reactions when they learned my family history and what I've encountered in my 15 years. I didn't exactly know what they were expecting at the time, but from the looks of it they sure as hell didn't get what they bargained for.

I propose that the foster care system be restructured into a real profession with high quality standards. In such a system, foster parents would need at least four years of *real* training. In short, they'd be taught what to expect from a foster child and how to deal with it.

If ACS doesn't wish to take on such a responsibility, then it shouldn't go about terminating biological parents' rights to their children without having made every possible effort to keep the family together.

Come on, folks. Let's start thinking about honesty and stability. After all, we are children (real-life children), not mail-order packages. We are fragile and need to be handled with care.

Baudilio wrote this story when he was 15. He went on to graduate from high school and attend college.

Walter Moore

Too Many Schools

By Akeema Lottman

I can remember clearly the day when I interviewed at The Secondary School of Journalism Academy. This school, if I got accepted, would be my fourth high school in four years.

I was tired because I'd already moved twice the previous year, which meant having to go to two different schools during my junior year. I hoped that maybe I would be accepted into this school because I loved to write.

The principal didn't make it easy. She looked over my transcripts, and decided that I should be placed in the 11th grade again. My heart sank as tears welled up in my eyes and the walls of my esophagus got tighter, making it impossible for me to swallow. There was no way in the world I was going to repeat 11th grade.

I began to cry right then and there as I pleaded for her not to do that. I told her I'd been in foster care since birth and moved around a lot. I also told her that my medical condition had put me in the hospital and forced me to miss weeks of school several times over the past two years.

The last time I got really sick, I hadn't received home instruction from the school for almost two months. I don't think my agency acted quickly enough to get my schoolwork to me, and since I'd recently transferred, the school didn't know me and hadn't made much effort to get things going. All of that had messed up my credits.

I asked the other teens in my house if being in foster care has caused them problems in school. They all said yes.

The principal just listened and finally said, "OK." Not a sympathetic "OK," more like an "alright, whatever" OK. I knew she didn't care for me as a student; I was just going to be another name on the school's roster. She and her secretary exchanged a few words and then her secretary looked at me and said, "Be here tomorrow at 8."

The next morning, I got my schedule. First period was gym. I walked into the gym and 60 eyes were on me—30 strangers whose faces all looked alike. My heart began to race as I took the long journey to the gym teacher's office.

English followed, and, like gym class, all eyes were on me. I gave the teacher my schedule and said that I was new. He asked for my name and it seemed like the whole room got quiet, waiting for my answer. My whole mouth got dry as I whispered, "Akeema."

The rest of the day was the same. In my other schools they had at least introduced me to the class, but here the teachers just wrote down my name, told me to take a seat and went back to the chalkboard to complete the lesson. They didn't seem to care at all. I felt mad lonely and lost as my peers stared at me, wondering who I was.

As the weeks went on I felt more and more like an outcast.

My junior classes were the only classes I enjoyed because the juniors were friendlier. Even though I only spoke to the same two people all day, I was just glad there was somebody. I hated going to my senior classes because I was alone. They all stared, but never once bothered to try to talk to me.

What I went through is common to a lot of teens in foster care who move around a lot. I decided to ask the other teens in my house if being in foster care has caused them problems in school. They all said yes. One of them wrote me this note:

"I am 16 and I belong in the 11th grade, but I am in the 9th grade with one or two credits. It's almost the end of the school year and I don't think I'm going to make it to the next grade by the fall. What do you think I should do?"

Then there's my brother. He comes home every day shouting, "I'm not going back to school!" and threatening to drop out. He's 19 and still in high school because his credits also got messed up with all the moving around, and they held him back a year. I guess sometimes dropping out seems like the easier route for him because he doesn't have a support system to fall back on.

One thing I've learned is that I have to be an advocate for myself.

But even though we're all struggling, we really do push ourselves. There were times where I had to take two classes on Saturday, two night school classes, and a zero (extra) period just to make up classes and receive credits after I'd moved again.

The foster care system should do more to help kids in care graduate. I also think teachers should reach out to new students. When you're new, you can't form that student-teacher bond like someone who's attended the school since their freshman year. If teachers could have one-on-one talks with new students, they could build trust and good relationships.

But I believe the students themselves should play a strong

role also. One thing I've learned is that I have to be an advocate for myself. My social workers and the other adults in my life haven't really pushed the school officials, so I've started taking initiative by asking more questions at school and asking for help again and again.

It's good if you already have supportive adults tackling these obstacles with you, but if you don't, it's important to let others know what you need. Having even one teacher or other staff member by your side can make a big difference. I wish I'd known that sooner.

Last August, I got the chance to speak on a panel of teens at a conference of lawyers and judges who wanted to know how being in foster care affects success in school.

Another girl on the panel made a big impression on me. She'd missed a lot of school growing up, too, but despite her trials and tribulations she made it into Yale University.

Her story really inspired me because she broke that stereotype that youth in care are going to be nothing but failures. I think stories like hers will begin to change people's attitudes. I hope that the lawyers, judges, and social workers at the conference learned that all of us on the panel are strong and motivated, and that we're fighters. None of us had given up.

Three weeks after I spoke on that panel, I received my diploma. I didn't walk down the aisle with the rest of my classmates, but it was still the best day of my life. I had pushed myself into graduating and believing that I could because I knew that no one else was going to do it for me. I didn't want the easy way out.

Now I'm ready to move on and really begin my life. I took the first step by applying and getting into Kingsborough Community College.

I'm excited about starting college, but I also worry that my experiences in high school might be repeated. I've heard a lot of people complain about how colleges don't understand the problems of students in foster care.

But I refuse to let these kinds of problems stop me. I want to further my education and begin my career. This time I'll be better able to advocate for myself by building relationships with my teachers and classmates and being persistent. This time, I won't try to do it all alone.

Akeema was 18 when she wrote this story.

Karolina Zaniesienko

Getting the Education You Deserve

By Akeema Lottman

While writing about my struggle to graduate (see the previous story), I was invited to speak on a panel with other teens in foster care and share my experience with a room full of lawyers, social workers, and judges. These were the people who had the power to change laws and stand up for kids in foster care so that we get the education we're entitled to.

Participating in the panel was a good experience. I found out that there are people who can help you and who will actually listen to you. One of the other speakers was Kathleen McNaught, director of the American Bar Association's Legal Center for Foster Care and Education. I interviewed McNaught to learn about educational rights of students in foster care.

Q: What are some common problems faced by youth in care when it comes to completing their education?

A: I think changing schools is a huge issue all across the country for young people in care. Kids in care often have to change schools a lot. It can keep them from graduating on time and from bonding with teachers, friends and peers.

When school changes are made, it's important to make sure that kids are immediately enrolled in the new school without long delays. The old and new schools should be communicating right away so that records and credits get transferred quickly.

Changes in living circumstances and in schools are often abrupt and without warning. We talk to a lot of young people who end up losing credits because they had to move suddenly. They might have even finished three and a half months of a four-month semester, but because they weren't there for the last couple of weeks, they end up not getting credit for a class.

Q: How exactly do problems with transferring credits or coursework lead to higher dropout rates?

A: Like most students, youth in care have goals to graduate and attend college. Unfortunately, changing schools often causes them to lag behind their peers. When foster youth are unable to earn credits for classes or coursework they've already completed, they fall behind on graduation requirements and may be held back. That's frustrating, and teens often lose the motivation to continue with school.

Q: Is anything being done about those problems?

A: A 2008 law called the Fostering Connections to Success and Increasing Adoptions Act is making big changes in the child welfare system. One of those changes involves trying to help students stay in school and graduate on time.

Under the new law, when an agency is placing a child in foster care (or changing a child's placement), the agency must take into account where the child is going to school and how close the new placement is to that school. That's important because school changes can be avoided altogether if your new placement can keep you in the same school.

If there's a good reason why a student should switch schools, the school system and the child welfare agency must make sure the student gets immediately enrolled and transfer all school records. Some states already have their own timelines for this. But the Fostering Connections law could require states to do it faster than they do now.

Q: Students often feel like they don't have much control over the decisions being made about their education. How can we advocate for ourselves?

A: If adults don't know your interests and strengths, it's very hard to make a good decision on your behalf. You need to have your voice heard, and it's important to be persistent in making the adults in your life pay attention. If you tell your caseworker there's a certain class you want to take and your caseworker ignores you or doesn't act on it, be sure to tell others: teachers, lawyers, foster parents, even the judge at a court hearing.

Tell people you have an opinion about where you should live, what classes you go to, and what goals you have for the future.

I feel strongly that when you are comfortable and interested in doing so, you should be attending your court hearings. It's a great opportunity to speak up about any issue that you feel is not being addressed by the people around you.

Q: Where else should you speak up?

A: Young people should also be participating in all meetings about planning. If an education meeting is going on, make sure you're being invited. If not, ask why you're not being included. Tell people you have an opinion about where you should live, what classes you go to, and what goals you have for the future.

If you can't be part of those meetings, make sure there's someone in the meeting who knows how you feel and who will be your advocate. You should have a say in which adults are going to make the best decision for you.

Q: I've heard that having a connection with one supportive adult at your school can make a big difference. Do you have any advice about how to find someone like that?

A: I think youth are often cautious (and understandably so) about sharing details of their lives with people at school. It's important to feel that this information is going to be handled in an appropriate and private manner. A good starting point is to work on developing trust with one adult at school so that you feel comfortable sharing information about your personal situation.

Akeema was 18 when she conducted this interview.

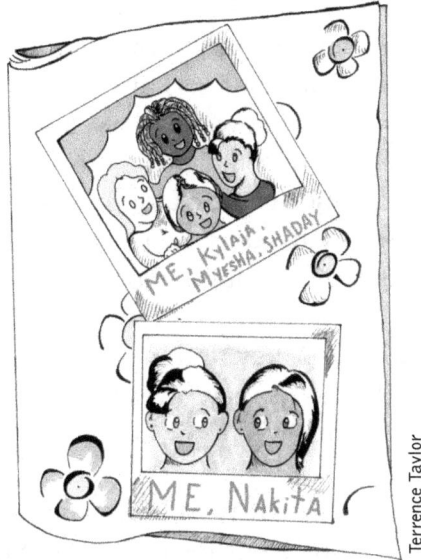

Terrence Taylor

Hard to Say Goodbye

By Sherelle Leggett

Sixth grade started on a beautiful September day a couple of days after my birthday. I can truly say I love school (which makes some kids look at me like I come from a different planet). But that year I was repeating 6th grade so I was type quiet. I was embarrassed that I had to do it over and I didn't know anyone in that grade.

When we got our assigned seats for the year, I was put next to a girl named Myesha. She was light-skinned and pretty with slanted eyes. I thought she must be conceited.

But at lunch we were assigned to a table together with two other girls from our class and we started talking. Shaday was pretty too, behind the glasses. She was kind of calm and she hated trouble. The other girl was Kylaja—she was hyper and made me laugh with her jokes and sarcastic ways.

I was the shy one so I was hardly saying anything. But I was happy to meet some new people. I was tired of seeing the same faces every day in my household. That's why I loved school.

Day by day we got to know each other. We started hanging out after school, just chilling like any other preteens. My foster mom was really strict and wouldn't let them come over, so I had to go over to where they lived in the projects in Queens.

I really didn't like to be around a lot of people, so my friends introduced me to everyone, which I thought was so caring. I got to know their families and they told me stories. I felt like we were all family. If I wasn't with Shaday I was with Kylaja, if not Kylaja I was with Myesha, whenever I got the chance to see them. We were like sisters.

I had a real sister, too, but we'd been separated since I was 9 and she was sent to a different foster home. Without my sister, I had to stick up for myself all those years. I always felt that I had to prove myself to people at such a young age. I felt that I couldn't talk to anybody, and I really felt alone. I didn't stay in touch with my sister or any of my siblings, because I didn't have their phone numbers and when I did speak to them it always made me cry.

I felt so not wanted at times. But I always thought that I shouldn't complain because there are a whole lot of kids suffering worse than me. I kept all my troubles and burdens to myself. Most times I acted out my anger in school with my fellow classmates who picked on me. But with Myesha, Shaday, and Kylaja I had some friends I could trust with my problems. At that time I felt that they were the only ones around me who cared.

It's a good feeling to know that you have friends. You get to let out your sense of humor. And when I got into problems with my foster mom I would call them or go to their house or we'd just chill outside for a little while.

My foster mother and her kids were mean to me, always

hitting me and punishing me for no reason. I felt like I was by myself in a family full of people that were all against me. It came to the point when I would just cry all the time and I even started thinking about killing myself. I didn't want to be on earth anymore.

My friends were the ones who told me, "Don't do that to yourself, just because your foster mom is doing you wrong. You've got a life ahead of you—don't waste that."

I used to hate going back into that house. But my friends were my getaway. They were the only ones who really cared about my feelings and basically the only ones to believe in me when I was told that I was nothing. They always said, "One day you'll get through this," and, "It's going to be OK." You know, nice stuff like that. They used to say, "I wish you could live with me." That made me cry.

My friends were my getaway. They were the only ones who really cared about my feelings.

We had our ups and downs, but we really cared about each other, and that's the only thing that mattered to me.

Then one summer day Myesha told us that she was moving to the Bronx. We were unhappy that the four of us wouldn't be together anymore, but she said that she would come back to visit. I was sad because she was the one I could really relate to, because some of her siblings were in foster care and she was sad about that. I didn't drop down crying when she said that she was moving, but when she left I sat in my room and listened to the song "It's so Hard to Say Goodbye," by Boyz II Men.

Myesha came back to visit on the weekends sometimes, and on her birthday we chilled in the Bronx and had fun. Later on when she went out with her family I stayed there with Shaday and Kylaja. We joked around and played Double Dutch.

Then I moved to Laurelton, Queens, and we all really lost contact with each other. My new foster mother was strict and didn't like me hanging out outside the neighborhood. Plus I couldn't always use the phone to call my friends, and they weren't able to call me either. Nobody had my new address, so one thing led to another and we fell out of touch.

Myesha, Shaday, and Kylaja were there when I really needed them, and not having them in my life anymore made me upset. I'd never had friends that I really loved like them before. I didn't have anyone to share my story with except them.

I didn't want to trust another person with my secrets and then wind up losing contact.

After that I had other friends and they were cool, you know, the usual. But something always passed me by about Myesha, Shaday, and Kylaja, wondering if they were OK. I thought that I'd never have friends like that again.

Myesha didn't like taking pictures but I'd taken a picture of her when she wasn't looking. I also got a few pictures of Shaday, and I had a little sticker picture of Kylaja. Every time I thought about them I'd look at those pictures.

I didn't want to call anyone else my best friend because I didn't want to trust another person with my secrets and then wind up losing contact. So I stopped having close friends for a while. I didn't want to go through the disappointment again.

A couple of years later, I met a girl named Nakita who lived across the street from me. We became friends after my foster mother invited her to a surprise birthday party she had for me. Nakita was really cool and nice. We went places together and joined the same dance school. But I still had that feeling about not trusting someone to be my best friend.

One day I was on the phone with her and she said something about best friends, and it startled me. I really did want to become her best friend, but something in me was like, "No, don't do it, she's going to leave like the others."

But a couple of months later I became real close to her. When you're around someone every day you start to get comfortable, and I decided to take that chance and make her my best friend.

I used to go over to her house all the time, and sometimes she would come over to mine if it was OK with my foster mother. We couldn't walk off the block most of the time and we used to hate that, especially when it was a hot summer day.

I started to get close to her family, too. Nakita and I told each other everything and I felt if I was ever to fall down she would help me get back on my feet. I had a lot of trust in her and I know she felt the same.

Then one day my foster mother and I got into a fight and she had me removed from her house the following day. While I was packing my things I started crying because I was scared of where I was going to end up and how I was going to tell my best friend.

I told Nakita and we were both upset, but I had to go. I said my goodbyes and as we drove off I said to myself, "Another friend down the drain." Tears flowed down my face like a waterfall and my eyes were heavy like rocks. I couldn't get a grasp on what was going on. I was mad at the whole world because I was leaving my best friend.

But this time, to my surprise, we kept in touch. We couldn't visit each other (I was at a diagnostic residential center), and for the first few weeks I couldn't call anybody. But we would send pictures and letters telling each other how we were doing. At the end of her first letter she wrote, "Love, your best friend." That's when I really believed in our friendship.

But I'm starting to realize that when people leave your life, you can find new people to come in.

Now it's two years later and Nakita and I are still close, even though we don't live near each other. We still call each other and joke around. I visit her most of the time because her mother won't let her come to Yonkers, but besides that everything is great.

Nothing changed between us—we have fun and have each other's backs. We speak to each other, if not every day, then every week. She cares for me the same way my old friends did, and she gives me a lot of support.

I still think about my old friends every time I look through my photo album and reminisce. When friends leave they take a part of you and you don't even know it. But I'm starting to realize that when people leave your life, you can find new people to come in.

Sherelle was 16 when she wrote this story.

Walter Moore

Torn Apart

By Anonymous

Carried nine months by a drug-addicted mother, I was born into a house where I was only as good as her next fix. I don't know what neighborhood we lived in. I only remember the reeking smell of piss in the hallway of our project, leaks in the ceiling, cracks in the wall, no heat in the winter and no AC in the summer. My little brother and sister and I slept on the floor because we had no bed to call our own. Our fridge was as empty as a poor man's pocket. Our mother never cooked for us; we survived on the scraps of food that she left.

Stepping on needles and glass in my mom's old apartment, the cuts on my feet bled like the scars from my heart. I wanted my mother to love me, but her addiction consumed her. It was more powerful than her love for her own kids.

As a young child I wasn't aware that my surroundings were

unusual. When I think back on the other kids in our building, I realize we weren't the only ones suffering with a parent's addiction. People were getting mugged and beaten in the stairwell, so the cops stayed in our building like it was a police station. And in our home, drugs were an everyday object.

As I got older, the greed of my mother's addiction grew. When she could not get her fix, or when she was forced to go sober from the lack of cash, she would hit us with a broomstick, extension cord, or anything else that she could get her hands on. She was desperate to find some way to forget about her own problems, something that would give her a rush.

The only time that our mother was able to show emotion and give attention to her kids was when she was abusing us. Otherwise, she showed us no feelings, no love. We were like rodents, scrambling around to pick up her scraps of food and trying to stay out of her way. I was hurt and confused. I thought, "How could she do this to her own kids?" After a while my heart got numb. I felt no hate toward her, but I also felt no love.

My brother and sister and I became closer than the average siblings because we had to look out for each other in order to survive. In the beginning there wasn't much I could do to protect them from my mom's abuse. I couldn't even protect myself. But we would do little things to try to comfort each other. Like if my sister was beaten, I would take the leftover food and give it all to her.

Then, when I was 7, my mother's addiction got so bad that she could not support her habit and maintain an apartment. She got evicted, and we followed her to a shelter in Brooklyn. The shelter was scary. I remember people stealing from each other.

I don't know how much time passed, maybe a few weeks. But one warm day, we went out with our mother and she just walked away from us. We didn't follow her, because we thought that she would be coming back. But she never did. After a while, we started getting hungry. We didn't know what to do. We didn't know how to get back to the shelter. That's when survival mode kicked in.

I'd never been able to depend on my mother, so I didn't really miss her when she disappeared. My main concern was getting us something to eat. When it got dark, we started walking. When we saw the projects, I thought we were home, but they weren't the same ones we'd lived in with our mom. We didn't know were else to go, so we followed someone into the building, cuddled up together on the floor and went to sleep.

From that day on, we were on our own on the streets. Like animals in the wild, we had to adapt to our environment. There were many nights we went hungry so we stole food, slept on the sidewalk and begged for money. But when people would just pass by, it made me cold-hearted. I felt no love, no joy, no happiness toward or from those who walked by.

One warm day we went out with our mother and she just walked away from us.

I started to feel helpless but besides that, my feelings were very limited. Except toward my brother and sister. They were a warm part of my heart, just a different part of me. Only they held the keys to my emotions.

We lived in filth, totally alone on the street. We had nothing but the clothes on our backs, which also served as blankets as it got colder. My brother wasn't potty trained, so he would defecate anywhere. Obviously we couldn't afford to buy him diapers.

We would wash ourselves in the McDonald's bathroom sink. Sometimes we'd even sleep in restrooms at McDonald's, Burger King or other fast food restaurants. Sometimes customers would kick us—literally kick us—to get us out of the restroom. As far as I know, no one ever checked to see if we had an adult looking out for us. Sometimes we'd lock ourselves in the restroom to sleep for a while, and the employees would unlock the door with their keys. Again, no one asked if we had a parent. They just told us to leave and sent us back out into the street.

Other times we'd take shelter inside the projects. We'd wait in the shadows and after a person entered the building, one of us would quietly come forward and hold the door. The other two of us would run in and we'd spend the night on the stairs or in the hallway. It really wasn't any better than sleeping in the restroom at McDonald's, because the stairs were full of places where people had pissed. We'd have to find a place to lie down where there was no piss, but the smell still invaded our air and made it difficult to sleep. And when winter came, it was cold sleeping on the floor.

We went to different stores each night to steal food, moving carefully so we wouldn't be noticed. We'd put the food items in our pants and shirts, and while the cashier was dealing with a customer, we'd walk out.

We couldn't really steal from McDonald's and KFC, so we'd wait till the end of a shift when they dumped food out and we ate out of the garbage. This was very dangerous, because we were competing with other homeless people, mainly adults, who hadn't eaten in days.

At first, it was hard to let go of the past. As rough as our lives had been before, I still had hope of finding our mom. But after a while I had to give up the past. If you don't stay focused on the present in circumstances like that, you're setting yourself up for failure, because you're distracted from what needs to happen right now in order to survive. Getting caught wasn't an option. Only our survival.

I never saw caring for my siblings as a short-term responsibility. I took it as a permanent responsibility, in place of a mother and father. I was the authority, but we needed each other to survive. They depended on me to make strategies and come up with plans for how we were going to eat and where we were going to sleep, to find something to wear and to protect them. I depended on them for motivation, which helped me protect not only them but myself.

My brother and sister gave me a strong will and something to believe in when I didn't believe we'd make it. They helped me find courage; I had to be strong for them. When I had a cold heart, they kept me warm inside. For their sake, I learned to numb my feelings when I was hurting. This was important, because if I had spent time getting attached to other people, or feeling hurt when other people mistreated us, I wouldn't have had the energy to keep going. Instead, I just focused on my brother and sister, and did everything for them. That was how I survived.

It was a good home, but I tried to sabotage it because I just wanted to be back with my siblings.

For months we lived this way, until my brother got caught stealing one summer day. His ribs were sticking out, dried spit crusted on his mouth from dehydration, wearing two different shoes on his feet and no shirt. The sun's heat blazed on his skin as he ran out of a nearby corner store with stolen goods.

The patrolman spotted him running down the street with one kids' size 11 boot and another size 6 toward the building where my sister and I were waiting. The door was cracked, and when my brother went to open the door he got caught. That's when the patrolman discovered the rest of us and we got pulled into the system.

When they explained what would happen to us next, I was relieved. We were going to have clean clothes, food, and a roof over our heads. I felt like I was in heaven, but little did I know that the physical and mental abuse would regenerate itself.

We lived in a group home for children for a while and were then placed in foster home after foster home, about 12 altogether. A lot of these homes were physically abusive. I remember that they'd treat their own kids good while they'd smack and hit us—sometimes with belt buckles—and tell us we weren't worth nothing.

Finally, when I was about 13, we found a good foster home. Our foster mother showed us love and compassion. She never called us nasty names or beat on us.

I wasn't used to kindness from an adult, because I'd been abused all my life. I couldn't let her love me. Her love felt different, it felt like something was missing. In fact, something was being gained, but I couldn't see it at the time. I'd never known an adult to give me love.

My foster mother finally had to let me go because I kept pulling away and her love couldn't hold me. Abuse had broken my heart into a million pieces and she tried to put it together, like a puzzle. But my hatred for my past foster families who abused me and used me for the money made me sink like an anchor, and I drowned in sorrow.

She couldn't handle me, so I was moved to another foster home. It was a good home, but I tried to sabotage it because I just wanted to be back with my siblings. I'd start fires, or drink too much alcohol so that the ambulance would have to come and take me to the hospital.

My behavior finally caused me to be placed in a residential treatment center. I didn't realize that the only thing that kept me strong, my siblings, would be taken away from me. If I'd known, I would have done anything in my power to keep them in my life.

At first I kept in touch with my brother and sister. But one day, about six months after I moved to the RTC, I called the house and no one called me back. I called again and the answering machine said they no longer lived there. I was so shocked and disturbed. Why would someone want to keep me away from my brother and sister?

As I got older, I tried to find a way to contact them, but I got nowhere. My law guardian explained that they'd been adopted by my former foster mother, so their file was confidential. They weren't allowed to give me any information about my brother and sister. I was hurt. I continued trying to find them by looking up their names and the foster mother's name on the computer, but I had no luck.

In the process of writing this story, I suddenly realized that my brother and sister are now teenagers. It was the first time I'd thought of them that way; in my mind, they were still children. When I realized they were teenagers, my first thought was, "That's crazy." I started thinking about my sister with a boyfriend and how I would act. How would I explain to my little brother about protecting himself and practicing safe sex? How would they manage without me there as a positive authority figure? Who did they call on when they needed help?

I also wonder if they think about me. I want to know if they miss me, if they feel the same way about me as I feel about them. Knowing that they're alive gives me hope, but not knowing what's going to happen to them worries me very much. If they died, I wouldn't even know. If I found out years later, me not being there would hurt me even more.

My childhood was nonexistent, and I can never get it back. Too young, I had to face the cold reality of the streets. Even though I'm 19 now, I can't help but let out the inner child sometimes. I try to be serious, but my vibe and my energy change the mood with people around my age. Some people think there's something wrong with me, but I'm just trying to get back something that was taken.

The picture in my mind is still of my brother and sister with me, frozen in our childhood years. I haven't been able to put an updated picture in the frame. I dwell on my childhood, always wondering about what I was like as a kid. The only two people who shared those times were my brother and sister. Without them, I'll never have a complete picture of who I was then.

The author was 20 when he wrote this story.

Paul John Paredes

Keep Me in Da Hood

By Sylinda Sinkfield

In foster care, I had the experience of being placed in my neighborhood and being placed away from home. After going through both, I believe that it's a good idea for children to be placed in the same neighborhoods they came from. When I was in care, I didn't want to move away from my friends, family, or my block.

When I was first taken away, I was only 7 years old. (I'm 18 now.) I was sent from home to home all throughout the five boroughs of New York City until I was moved back into my old neighborhood in Manhattan. I was happy to be back and even happier that my sisters and brother were going to be staying in the same foster home. They were all I had.

At first it was hard because my siblings and I were told that we couldn't go see our mother. The funny thing was that our mother lived in the building right across the street! But I was happy that I would at least be able to be near my mother, even if I couldn't see her.

We also knew the lady that we were staying with, so that made things better. I was able to go back to my old school and be around my friends. Your friends are important at times when you're down; they're the ones who make you feel better. I needed my friends around.

Being in the same neighborhood made it easier to pretend nothing was happening. I knew this wasn't so, but it was better than facing the truth. My mind wouldn't let me understand that something was wrong. It just felt like my mother went somewhere and left me at a friend's house for a very long time.

It hurts like a sharp pain when the world you once knew is not the same anymore.

I believe this type of environment was best for me. I was 7 years old, scared, and had no clue. Living in my neighborhood, I didn't have to go through a lot of major changes. I could walk down the street and see people I knew.

Don't get me wrong—it wasn't as easy as I thought. I was still without my mother. But at the same time I got support from my friends, my school, and my neighborhood.

The second time I got taken away I was 11 or 12. I was living in the Bronx at the time. It was hard for me to leave because I had to say good-bye to all my friends. I was first placed in a foster home in Manhattan and later was moved to Queens. I didn't know a thing about Queens.

Not only was I not in the same neighborhood, but I also wasn't with my brother and sisters, and that made the experience like hell. My foster family and I didn't get along, and I hated the area. There was nowhere to go, there were no stores around, and there was nothing there that reminded me of home. I felt so left out and so uncomfortable that I began to lash out at my foster mother. I was so unhappy.

When I returned back home to the Bronx one year later, everything in my old neighborhood had changed. The world that I once knew was gone, including my best friend from the sixth floor. There were new faces in almost all the apartments. It hurts like a sharp pain when the world you once knew is not the same anymore.

I know many of you have run away from your foster home or group home to go back to your old neighborhood, to be around faces you recognize. If you're placed in the same neighborhood, you might know the person that you're going to be staying with. It may not even seem as if you were just taken away. It's already hard that you lost your mother or father and siblings. Being around your friends and your surroundings can make it easier for you to adjust to what's happening.

But there are people who disagree with me and say it's not a good idea to be placed in your old neighborhood. They say you shouldn't be put in the same place that you were just taken away from, because the surroundings must not have been the best for you in the first place. I think it depends on your situation.

For me, it was better to be in a familiar place. If I had to be in foster care, I'd rather be around at least one thing that is familiar to me—and not just a bunch of strangers.

Sylinda was 17 when she wrote this story.

Rosheed Wellington

Goodbye, Harlem

By Antwaun Garcia

I met my boy when I was 8. He was shy and something of a follower, but cool. If I cut school, he would cut with me. If I went to the candy store, he'd buy candy if he had money or he would take it.

My boy was growing up a lot like me—on the streets all times of the night, not wanting to go home. Some days his father would hit him, or my boy and his siblings wouldn't eat, because even when their moms was sober and wanted to cook, she couldn't afford food. We became Robin Hoods, stealing from the Bravo store to feed the poor.

I wasn't thrilled about stealing to eat, but it was so easy to do it became a habit. We would walk in the store and act like family, yelling, "Mommy wanted this!" Or, "Moms needed bread for sandwiches in the morning." He would put a few items under his shirt.

I would walk out first and wait for the "walk" sign. As soon as the light changed, I would open the door and he would run right through and across the street into my building.

We had tons of fun together, playing sports, chilling on the park benches eating stolen food, and laughing it all off. Even though our situation wasn't good, we found ways to enjoy life.

But when I was 10, I went into foster care and moved to Queens, New York, with my aunt. Moving to Queens was so unexpected I didn't have a chance to say goodbye to him or any of my friends. Later, I wondered about him and all my family. I missed being home and wondered how they were holding up.

When I arrived in Queens, I felt very weird. My aunt lived in a housing development with security and, between each group of four buildings, a huge circle of flowers and sprinklers. I'd never seen flowers like that in my old neighborhood, Harlem. Maybe once in a blue you would see some dude selling roses on a street corner, rolling to your window and saying, "Flowers, flowers for your loved one." But that was it. In Queens, I felt like Dorothy in "The Wizard of Oz." I just clicked my shoes three times and I was in paradise.

Still, adapting to my new home was really difficult. My aunt had rules like, "Be home at dark." I thought, "What? Home by dark?" I was used to coming home at midnight. I also had to do chores and homework, be in bed by 9, and attend school daily, which was new for me. I hated it from the jump.

The biggest change was emotional. Even though I was safe, I always had this feeling that someone was going to double-cross me and I stayed cautious, my hands ready to swing. I didn't know how to react to courtesies, like someone holding doors for me or saying, "Good morning, have a nice day!" I was like, "Uh, duh...OK! Whatever!"

In Harlem, people weren't nice to me unless they knew me or my relatives. It took me a while to realize that, surprisingly, the nice people in Queens didn't have a hidden agenda.

I also found myself acting like I was back in the ghetto even though I had everything I needed. I'd steal food from stores when I had food in the house, or sell weed and bootleg CDs to make some money even though I didn't need to. I couldn't seem to get hustling out of my system. I still enjoyed the thrill and excitement of possibly getting caught, and I didn't want to lose my game. I never knew if I'd end up back in Harlem again, taking care of myself.

Living with my aunt, I also felt isolated. I felt I couldn't trust anyone and had no one to really talk to. My aunt's family acted stubborn and proud, and made fun of each other for being dumb or making mistakes. I feared they thought they were too good for me. I never felt comfortable enough around them to tell them what I felt, so I kept to myself.

He had stayed behind in Harlem, and his Harlem had been what it was for me: Crack, poverty, drugs, 5-0, and violence.

The older I became the colder my heart became. For years, I isolated myself from all of my family. I barely went back to Harlem to see my extended family or my old friends. I missed my mother and father, but I was also angry at them for letting me end up in care and for being out of touch for long periods of time.

Instead, I just kept my head down and tried to take what Queens offered me. In school, I finally learned to read and write. Later I became a writer at *Represent*, a magazine for teens in foster care. I earned my diploma, started an associate's degree and began to believe I might make it as a journalist or working in the music industry. Slowly, I began to see myself not as a kid who would need to hustle his way through life, but as someone who could make it.

When I was in high school, I started feeling comfortable taking the train back to Harlem. One afternoon when I was 18, I saw my boy and his fam. As I approached him and his uncle on the steps of his building, they said, "Yo, that's Twaun. What's good, son?"

They sounded excited to see me, but the way my boy paved greeting to me was funny. He gave me a fake pound, a quick slap, like, "Don't touch my hand." At first I didn't pay any mind to it. I was happy to see my people.

We started talking about what had been going on in the 'hood since I left. It was the same sad violin story: a couple of people locked up, some shot, some on crack, and a bunch either in foster care or dead. I kept my head down for a moment thinking about what they went through. It hurt.

We were quiet for a moment looking around the block. I asked my boy, "What you been up to, fam?" He said, "Nothing. Same old @#$%, different day."

I started telling him that I'd just achieved my high school diploma and planned to go to college, and that I wrote for *Represent*, trying to make big moves.

Judging by his facial expression, he wasn't too thrilled to hear I was becoming successful. I noticed his posture changed and his tone got more serious. He eyed my fresh gear, my lion piece chain, the three rings on my fingers, and the earrings that were shining more than 42nd Street at night. I guess he assumed I was caked up.

Then he tried to clown me in front of his brother and uncle, saying, "Oh word, so you doing your thang." He laughed like my goals in life were something humorous to him, like I was some stuck up punk from the suburbs who wasn't 'hood enough to be back home.

He took another pull of his cancer stick and told his uncle, "Yo, this ain't the same little kid I know. This n-gga changed."

Then he got in my face and said, "You pussy! You ain't the same cold-hearted young n-gga who used to be real and hold @#$% down."

At first I thought he was joking, but he wasn't. His eyes were squinty and his cheek muscles were tight. I was caught off guard. I never thought my boy would attack my character or throw hands with me. I thought he would be happy to see me doing my thang.

I wanted to fix his lip. I was thinking, "We'll see how much I changed when I punch you in your mouth." I am a quick tempered dude but I fell back and kept my cool. Instead of applying physical force, I played the mental game.

I replied, "So what makes me different? Because now I have a little money in my pockets? Or because you still that same cat hustling for years with no bread, struggling to make ends meet and still eating off your mom's welfare check?"

He got upset, and I could tell his family didn't like my comment either. His younger

In Queens I'd gotten the chance to start a whole new life.

brother started to ball his fist as if to swing at me. But I continued, "Is it because you're still that same punk who needed me to fight your battles, take groceries from the store because your moms couldn't afford them?"

His uncle started cursing at me at the top of his lungs. "What! Who the @#$% are you to disrespect our family!" He wouldn't stop, saying every curse word in the book.

As soon as I began taking my coat off, preparing for someone to pop off, their moms came out. I felt bad for making that comment about her because she looked very ill and was coughing. She yelled, "Antwaun!" and gave me a hug and a kiss on the cheek. "Boy, I haven't seen you since you was that little angry, always fighting, peasy-headed kid, and now look at ya, you full grown and handsome."

I smirked while saying, "Thank you." She began telling me how hard it's been, especially since she'd been diagnosed with breast cancer. I could see the coldness in her brown eyes and hear the pain in her voice.

I felt for her. She was always cool with me. When her kids ate,

I ate too. When I wanted to get away from my house, she always said I could come through. She was funny and smart, just not smart about getting caught in the crack game.

Then the uncle came into our convo and told her that I wasn't allowed around here no more. I gave him a cold look as my teeth scraped each other like nails scraping the blackboard. I said, "Say no more!" I gave their mother a kiss on the cheek and said it was nice to see her after so many years. She replied, "The same with you, Antwaun. I am so proud of you!"

As I walked away, I felt upset that I had lost my boy who I had been cool with for years. Thinking it over, I realized that he wasn't jealous of me because of what I was wearing, but because of the goals and dreams I believed were possible.

He had stayed behind in Harlem, and his Harlem had been what it was for me: Crack, poverty, drugs, 5-0 and violence. Could I expect any more from him than to live up to his environment? Could I expect him to be happy for my good fortune when he wished to have the opportunities I was given? Don't get it twisted, I was not being cocky, but realizing I've been fortunate.

In Queens I'd gotten the chance to start a whole new life, including going to school and living in a positive environment where I felt the freedom to become more than a punk. He was stuck living a lifestyle that he didn't choose.

In the last few years, I've thought a lot about that last convo with my boy. As I get closer to aging out, it seems like I might end up moving back to Harlem. That feels weird, like I could wind up right back where I started, even though I've worked hard to be moving on up, as they said on the Jeffersons.

I wonder, "When I age out, will I become the educated and professional person I hope to be, or will I just go backwards?" I fear that, no matter how much success I may obtain, I could always fail at any moment.

What my boy couldn't see is that I still battle my own inner demons. I still carry around a 'hood mentality that makes me doubt I'll reach my dreams. Despite the hopeful picture I painted for my boy, it's hard for me to believe that long-term goals, like finishing college, will be things I'll live to achieve.

I often ask the people close to me, "Can I make it?" With reassurance from other people, I've started believing in myself, but it hasn't been easy. I'm not like many of the people I know from Queens or in college, who seem so confident of their futures.

But at least I know that hustling can never be a route to a good life. That right there should keep me on the straight path, safe from ever becoming the worst parts of the Harlem I grew up in.

Antwaun was 21 when he wrote this story.

Chris Pope

My Life on the Move (Again)

By Sharif Berkeley

I used to live in a group home in Hollis Park Gardens, in Queens, New York. It was a nice suburban neighborhood where I could sit outside my house and not have to worry about being robbed or shot. Every house that lined the street was beautiful, with manicured lawns and lots of trees.

I loved that area. This was a place where you could raise your kids and grow old without having to worry about who or what was outside the door. There were police cars parked on every block to keep the peace, plus all the people who lived there were wealthy and respectable.

I stayed at Hollis Park Gardens for about a year and a half before they broke the news to us that we had to move due to budget cuts. I was depressed because I had to leave an area I loved so much. I was proud of the fact that I had finally moved out of the ghetto, and now I was afraid of being thrown back in.

My next group home, the one I presently live in, is in East Flatbush, Brooklyn. I wasn't too crazy about moving to Brooklyn, but I had to deal with it. At least I was still in the same agency.

Luckily, three of my old staff members found their way to the group home that I was moving to. And I liked the new house. It was bigger than the one I moved from and my room was the largest bedroom I had ever seen (about the size of two living rooms in the projects).

I was proud of the fact that I had finally moved out of the ghetto, and now I was afraid of being thrown back in.

But the neighborhood of East Flatbush leaves much to be desired. The teenagers all act like hard rocks and I always have to watch my back. After two of them came out of a dark driveway one night and tried to rob me, I've been extra careful about where I walk and how late I stay out.

Then there are the private houses which are packed so close together, you could slap your next door neighbor if you were both hanging out the window.

After six months of living there, I've gotten used to my new residence. I thought I wouldn't have to move again, but my hopes didn't last. Because of more budget cuts, on June 15 we will not only have to move again, but be split up into other agencies.

This news was as bad as getting charcoal on Christmas. Each day I feel like I'm on death row, counting off the days one by one. With all these budget cuts, I have no faith in the foster care system. It's become a game of pool, and the city is the cue ball knocking us into the corner pockets.

This time I have been knocked into the pocket of the Green Chimney's agency in Manhattan. It's not that I wouldn't like to move to Manhattan, my favorite place. It's just that I won't be in my old agency with all the people I know. Moving is one thing, switching agencies is another. There will be a whole new set of social workers and staff to get used to all over again.

I now understand how hard it is for foster kids who get thrown around from place to place. I guess the only way to guarantee the end of my "rolling stone" syndrome would be to get a place to call my own.

Sharif was 15 when he wrote this story. He went on to graduate from high school and attend Lehman College.

Fernando Garcia

A Love Too Strong

By Tamecka Crawford

I had to fall flat on my face before I learned that I was alone in this world. I came from a home where there was no love shown, where at night I'd sit up in bed and cry because there was no one to give me a shoulder to lean on when I needed support, a pat on my back when I did something good, or even a sympathetic ear when I failed.

My father passed away when I was a child, and my step-mother simply never returned home one day. I went to live with my paternal grandmother and then a maternal aunt, but neither living situation worked out. It seemed like someone had cursed me, that there was a dark cloud hanging over my head.

Two years ago, at 16, I came to a group home in Queens. For the first time I met people who really cared about me, who accepted me without judgment, who gave me the love and attention I needed.

But the first few months at the home were hard. I was very scared. I didn't know how to act, whether or not to close myself off from people. Back home I was so used to nobody caring that I just stayed alone in my room. I wasn't used to receiving love and attention, but the staff made it hard for me to stay isolated.

The staff got involved in my everyday life. They were always interested in hearing about what was happening in school or my social life—things my family never asked about. We had Independent Living class once a week and the teacher always made it very interesting for all the girls. She would always ask us questions to get us to open up about our feelings.

One staff member in particular, Ms. Thomas, really touched my heart.

The first week I got to the group home, Ms. Thomas called a house meeting with all the girls. We discussed many things, such as the staff's behavior toward the girls, boyfriends, and age differences among the residents.

I didn't know how to act, whether or not to close myself off from people.

I can remember all 12 of us sitting around the living room. Ms. Thomas wanted us to talk one at a time, but every time someone spoke there were at least nine interruptions from people who disagreed. Ms. Thomas became very upset with our disrespectful behavior. Everybody was pointing at each other and getting overexcited, the phone kept ringing, and it was just crazy.

Suddenly Ms. Thomas began to cry. It was the first time I had ever seen anyone cry for someone else. It showed me how deeply she cared for us, how much it bothered her that we didn't care for anyone but ourselves.

Since I never had anyone take such an interest in me before, I began to admire Ms. Thomas dearly. The rest of the staff did nothing except what they were paid to do. But Ms. Thomas was always there to listen, to see how she could help me one way or another. She always encouraged us to visit our families and always checked up on how we were doing in school. I found myself getting very attached to her, but one day she was transferred from my house to another house within the agency.

When Ms. Thomas left, I closed myself up again. I began to stay to myself and hide in my room. I felt that Ms. Thomas was the only person who could ever take away my feelings of being unloved. She was the only one who accepted me as I was, who knew my needs as a child, and now she was gone.

The funny thing is, Ms. Thomas was unaware of how I felt about her, and when the staff told her how I had closed up again, she acted very cold-hearted whenever she saw me.

Like everyone else, Ms. Thomas felt I had become too dependent on her, that she could never be that "perfect mother figure" that I had imagined her to be. I didn't want her to be distant from me, I wanted her to love me back. I hated her for letting me down and hated myself even more, because I had no control over my feelings.

I was scared and I went through an emotional hell. I had flashbacks to the time I lived with my family, the time when nobody cared. My family felt that if I had a roof over my head and clothes on my back, there was no need to say "I love you." I dreaded the return of that lonely feeling.

Ms. Smith, director of social work, went to war with me over my attachment to Ms. Thomas. She kept reminding me that my attachment to Ms. Thomas was very unrealistic and that it was inappropriate for me to act and feel that way toward an agency staff member.

I despised her for telling me that. At times I knew deep in my heart that Ms. Smith was right and really cared about my well being, but I stood firm. I couldn't face being unloved again and I was terrified by losing Ms. Thomas. I was even more determined than ever to win Ms. Thomas' attention.

Until this day, I still admire Ms. Thomas. My feelings for her go up and down like a roller coaster. I realize that Ms. Smith was partly right, that my expectations were unrealistic and sometimes unfair. But on the other hand, my attachment to Ms. Thomas is just another bond that has been broken by the system. I was searching for love and attention, no matter how it came.

Ms. Thomas was the only one who accepted me as I was, and now she was gone.

As a victim of the foster care system, I have learned to never take anything for granted, that all my troubles are temporary, and that relationships aren't always permanent. I have learned not to count upon too many people, but to look within myself for guidance and security. That way, if anyone "disses" me I won't be disappointed.

I've learned to open up to those who are willing to open up to me, but at the same time not to mistake their kindness for a parent's love, a kind of love that can never be replaced.

Tamecka was 19 when she wrote this story.
She graduated high school and attended college.

YC Art Dept.

Fifteen Months in Care: And Fifteen Placements!

By Youniqiue Symone

I was in the system for 15 months, and during that time I moved to 15 different places (six foster homes, five group homes, two diagnostic centers, and two residential facilities). Yes, 15 different homes in 15 months!

Why was I moved to so many different places? Why didn't my social worker know what was going on with my case? Where was the help that the system promised me? And how many more times will this happen to a child before they realize that they are doing something wrong? These are the questions that run through my mind.

There are many reasons why I got moved 15 different times— my caseworker had too big a caseload to keep track of me, I was put into bad placements, and there was poor communication between my caseworker and me.

I went AWOL eight times because I felt I had no other choice. My living situations got so bad that I couldn't stand to be in them anymore. For example, my second foster mother, Ms. D, was always yelling at me because she wanted me to set an example for the other children in the house. After a while, she thought she could put her hands on me. When she hit me one night, we fought. I called my social worker and I told her I wanted to leave.

Now here is where my social worker should have stepped in, instead of making me go back to Ms. D's home. She said, "It's Friday, it's 5 o'clock. Wait until Monday."

My living situations got so bad that I couldn't stand to be in them anymore.

No foster child should be hit or hurt by their foster parent. No matter what time or day it was, I feel that my social worker should have moved me. I don't feel she should have sent me back to that home. If a child is getting hurt, something should be done right then and there. It should not wait.

Another foster mother, Ms. S, shouldn't have been a foster mother. She was always either at work or at the clubs. She was never home, and when she was, we would find strange men in the house. She would be drunk all the time.

That wasn't a healthy environment for me or the other foster children. I wasn't really worried about me or the oldest boy. I was more worried about the two youngest children (who were 8 and 11). They didn't need to see that.

Once again I explained this to my social worker, and once again I was moved. Meanwhile, Ms. S is still a foster mother and is doing the same things. I explained to my social worker that she shouldn't be a foster mother, because she was just in it for the money. My social worker said, "No, she's not. No one else seems to have a problem with her but you."

Next I was moved to a group home. My social worker was supposed to come and move me there, but once again one of her co-workers came to pick me up. I didn't understand why my social worker couldn't be there. This is another example of how my social worker lost track of my case.

After the first week the house started to fall apart. One of the girls wore a piece in her hair and she would leave it in the bathroom. So this attracted bugs. Then another girl did her hair in the bathroom and left gel all over the place.

Another girl had a turtle, but didn't want to keep the tank clean. So the water used to stink and turn colors. The same girl used to take off her clothes and leave them wet and dirty in a corner. So the upstairs used to stink, no matter how clean my room was.

I wanted to move but my social worker wouldn't let me. I had to go AWOL in order to be placed again. Had my social worker made surprise visits to the group home, then maybe my going AWOL could have been prevented.

In my second diagnostic center, I was wrongly accused of jumping another girl. When I had room detention, I asked why. No one would tell me. One of the staff let a girl get into a fight and just watched her get beat up. I explained that to my social worker. She said, "What do you want me to do? Just stick around for your last month and then you will be moved."

Then I went to my second residential facility. It was filthy. Staff were cursing at the residents. You had to worry about looking at another resident wrong. Even the staff were afraid. If they didn't like you, the kids wanted to start a fight.

I was only in there for three days and a staff got stabbed. Another resident got shot. Every day there was a fight. A boy got beat with a stick and had to be rushed to the hospital.

They were sending kids upstate left and right. It was really rough. I think my placement there could have been prevented had my social worker listened and talked with me, instead of not taking my phone calls. I didn't deserve to be in the placements I was in; no one did. I said enough is enough, so I went AWOL and left the system for good.

Living outside the system has been better for me then living in the system. Out of all my placements, only four were good, and I was taken from those four against my will.

When I told my social worker my problems, she should have come and helped me out, not told me try to "make it work." How can you try to make it work when you're scared for your life? I felt she was blaming me.

If I didn't have my lawyers (Nancy Dunbar, Andra Ramos) or my godmother (Malika Legrand), I don't know where I would be. The good people in the system have had such a big impact on my life. They have stuck behind me through thick and thin. I not only thank them, I also love them.

> *When I told my social worker my problems, she should have come and helped me out, not told me try to "make it work."*

Here are some suggestions that might prevent children from being moved so often:

• Childcare workers should not have such big caseloads. I feel they should only have 15 cases. That way they can keep track of the children and how they're doing.

• Staff need more training and I feel they should have a degree in childcare work. I also feel staff should be trained by residents as well as by other staff. Some staff are ignorant, and feel we are garbage because we're in the system.

• Social workers should make surprise visits, instead of calling the foster home or group home and letting them know they're coming. With surprise visits, the workers can really see the conditions in the house.

• When a child goes into the system, he or she should receive a booklet that describes in detail the child's rights in foster care and where to get help.

• There should be a 24-hour hotline that young people can call when they're having problems. Most problems don't happen during the 9 to 5 workday.

• Last, but not least, each child who enters the system should meet with their lawyer as soon as possible. I was never told I had a lawyer until my last few months in the system. My lawyers did the best they could, considering the lost time. If I had known I had a lawyer earlier, a lot of my problems might have been avoided.

We are the children who make up the system. It's not our fault that we're here, but we are. We are just like any other children. Just because we're not living at home, we shouldn't be treated differently. We want to be treated with respect and dignity.

Youniqiue was 16 when she wrote this story. She went on to graduate from high school and work in afterschool programs.

Christina Pacheco

Taken From a Home I Loved

By Charlene Johnson

I had just gotten out of school for the day. My twin sister Charlotte said she needed to go to the library to catch up on some work, so we called my foster mother to see if it was OK.

"Hello, may I please speak to Lorna," I said in a foreign accent. She always knew it was Charlotte or me when we did that and it always made her laugh.

"Yes, this is Lorna," she responded. I could sense that something was wrong by the way she answered me.

"And how are you today?" I asked.

"I'm OK," she answered.

"Lorna, Charlotte and I wanted to know if it was alright to go to the library?"

"No, come straight home."

"Please, we have to work on the report for school."

"Just come home," she said.

When Charlotte and I reached home, my foster mother was in the kitchen. She said she had to tell us something. At first I thought someone had called my house from school. I never expected what she was about to tell me and my sister.

"Girls," she started, "the social worker called me today and told me that you have to go and live with your little sisters in another foster home in Queens."

As she said that, it felt like someone stabbed a knife right in my chest. I knew that the system tries to keep families together, but it wasn't fair. I began to cry and then I ran upstairs to my room. I could hear my twin sister crying as well. We had been in Lorna's home for six months and now we had to move.

Soon Lorna came to our room to comfort us. I knew deep down inside Lorna wanted to cry also. But I also knew she wanted to be strong for us. All she kept on saying was that maybe it would be better if we lived with the other lady. She said, "Sometimes the grass is greener on the other side."

The rest of that day was hard for me. I couldn't focus right on anything but the fact that I would soon be leaving the

I would soon be leaving the woman I had grown to care for very deeply.

woman I had grown to care for very deeply. I thought Lorna really didn't worry that much until I saw her cry. Until this day I can see the tears running down her cheeks and her eyes turning red.

I can still remember how Lorna, my sister, and I held one another in that moment of everlasting sorrow. The pain you feel when you're torn apart from a loved one without any warning is the worst feeling a person can have.

My sister and I were L.J.'s (her full name is Lorna Joyce Winter) first foster children, and this was our first permanent foster home. We had been in the system for two months and in one emergency home before we came to Lorna's house. So we really didn't know how the foster care system operated. The three of us became very close.

Every evening at dinner we had a nice talk. Lorna is the type of person who liked to know what we were doing with our time. Not only did she listen to our problems and give us advice, but she also told us what was going on with her life and, if possible, we gave her some advice.

I'm not saying that we never had any mishaps with each other, but I am saying that if we did have any disputes we solved them in a reasonable manner. A child would be lucky to have Lorna as a mother because she's a caring, loving, understanding, giving, and patient woman. A nice person to talk with or have fun with, not to mention an excellent cook. So you can see why I didn't want to leave.

The day came when I had to go. When I was leaving, I couldn't stop the tears from coming. I cried all the way to the new home.

I felt bad until I saw my two little sisters there, Charmel and Charisse. They made me stop thinking about going back to live with L.J. I started to think maybe it was for the best and not the worst.

The new home was not what I expected. My first impression of the foster mother was that she was a nice lady. But as time went by, Mrs. B showed her true colors. It seemed like the longer I stayed, the less she fed me.

She treated my sister and me like little babies. She didn't let us do anything. I was supposed to be living there so I could see my sisters more, but that never happened. They had to be in their room and we had to stay in ours.

Every day was the same thing. I would get up, take a shower, eat breakfast with Charlotte (we couldn't eat with my sisters because Mrs. B didn't want us to talk) and go to school. Then I would come home and wait to pick my little sisters up from school. After that I ate dinner and got ready for school the next day.

After a while I was getting tired of this prison-type treatment. Something had to be done. So I decided to tell the social worker. I told her about the woman's cruelty. But would she listen and try to help me?

No, that was the last thing on her mind. She said she told the foster mother about my complaints. I really didn't believe that because there were no changes. If anything, it seemed to be getting worse.

I knew that nothing was going to get accomplished if I didn't take matters into my own hands. My sister and I decided to run away from the home. We knew exactly where we were going and how we were planning to do it. The next time Mrs. B sent us to the store would be the time to break away.

It was a bright and sunny spring day. Mrs. B sent Charlotte and me to pick up some milk and juice at the supermarket. We both knew what was in store for us when we stepped outside.

I was so frightened and nervous when my sister and I began to walk up the block. I wasn't sure if I wanted to go through with it (but a girl's got to do what a girl's got to do). We turned the corner at the Associated supermarket and made a phone call to one of my old friends. She wasn't home. We didn't know where to go until it hit me—my mother's house in Manhattan.

When we finally agreed on going to my mom's house, we walked as quickly as possible to the subway station. While walking, I noticed my sister kept looking over her shoulder. She said she was scared that we were going to get caught. I told her not to worry about it, that no one would catch us. And no one did.

I stayed at my mom's house almost two days. I really couldn't bring myself to stay there any longer because of the bad environment and the kind of company she was having, so I decided to give Lorna a call. Since moving to the new home, I'd been calling Lorna to keep her updated about what was happening.

When I called, Lorna was overjoyed to hear from me. She said that the new foster mother called her house a few times because she thought Lorna was hiding us.

Lorna told the two of us to come to her house. At first I thought it was a trick. Then I asked her if the social workers were going to be there to take us and she said no. I knew Lorna wouldn't lie to me, so I told her that I was on my way.

When I got to her house, Charlotte and I were kind of nervous to knock on the door because we didn't know who was in there. After standing outside the house for a good five minutes, I finally rang the bell. Lorna's grandson Danilo opened the door.

I could tell he was surprised to see us again. After he let the two of us inside, we both ran upstairs to Lorna's room. L.J. was lying down in her bed watching one of her evening programs. She didn't know we were standing there. Charlotte then said in a low voice, "Joyce, Joyce." Not knowing that it that it was my sister and me, Lorna said, "SSShhh! My show, my show."

If anyone had taken the time to speak to us, they would have found out that we didn't want to move.

At that moment Charlotte and I started laughing. Then Lorna realized who was standing in front of her bedroom door. Within five seconds Lorna was up out of the bed and hugging me and Charlotte. This was the best welcome I had in the last couple of months.

I felt so happy when I came to Lorna's house. I sincerely thought we were staying for good. I couldn't think of a place where I would rather be at that period of my life.

That evening the social worker called. She asked me why we ran away. I told her that I couldn't stand Mrs. B. When I told her that, she said something to me that was not necessary to say. She told me that Lorna was only in it for the money.

I couldn't believe what my ears were hearing. I thought if anyone was doing it for the money, it was Mrs. B.

The next day the social worker from Mrs. B's agency came

to take my sister and me back to the foster home. This time we didn't worry as much, because we knew we were coming back to L.J. soon. At least that's what my lawyer and the social worker at Lorna's agency said.

In two weeks, with the help of my grandmother and my lawyer, Charlotte and I were placed back with Lorna. We still live with her and we intend to stay with her until we leave care. I think this experience brought me closer to Lorna, and every day our relationship progresses.

The main problem I am trying to point out about foster care is their bad habit of moving children from home to home. I don't think they realize how much emotional stress they put on a child every time they place him in a different home.

Being moved is not fair to a child. She doesn't get the proper satisfaction of being in a home she can call her own, or ever feeling the love and security of a family. Isn't that the reason why children are placed in foster care?

In my case, I think the child welfare workers thought they were doing a good thing by moving Charlotte and me back with our sisters. But if they had actually taken the time to speak to us, they would have found out that we didn't want to move.

If child welfare workers talked to the children and found out what they really wanted, some of these moves could be prevented.

Charlene was in high school when she wrote this story.

Julio Juarez

My Foster Siblings:
They Come and They Go

By Ana Angélica Pines

My neighborhood has gone through a lot of changes since our family first moved there when I was 2. Most of the people who lived there back then have moved out, and there aren't as many trees as there used to be. But the biggest change has been inside people's homes. Starting when I was about 8, almost every family on my block began taking in foster kids. At first, most did it because of the money the government gives you to take care of them. But for some of us, it became more than that.

The first kid that ever came to my house was named David. He was 8 and I was 9. I didn't know exactly why he was living with us, but I knew he was a foster child. Because he was a boy, my brother started playing with him and forgetting about me and I couldn't help but get mad because I was a blood relative and then this strange kid came and started getting special attention. He also got to go to the store by himself and I would get pissed because, even though I was older, I wasn't allowed to do that. I remember arguing with my family about it. (I suppose I was a feminist even then.)

David was with us for a couple of months. We always went outside to play hide and seek with the other kids or go to the park with my mother or sister. But even if you treat kids like David well, most don't feel that they belong—no matter what you do. It's only natural for them to want to be with their biological families; I know I would.

During the short time David was with us, my mother used to talk on the phone with his grandmother. I remember one time he ran away and the police came to my house. Later, they found him at his grandmother's. In the end he went to live with her.

After David, my mother decided not to take any kids older than 5. That way at least we wouldn't have to deal with any more running away.

A lot of kids came and went after that. Two that stick in my mind were a sister and brother named Tashira and Brandon, ages 4 and 5. They were always fighting. Brandon would kick and scream in stores if he didn't get what he wanted—something my family wasn't used to because my siblings and I were all quiet kids. Finally, after a couple of months, my mother called the foster care agency and told them that we couldn't handle it, to take them back. It was a hard decision, but one that needed to be made.

I remember when the agency worker came to pick them up, Brandon started crying and screaming that he didn't want to go to another foster home. The agency worker told him that he wasn't; he was going to his mother's house. I knew she was lying. We had called the agency and if he was really being returned to his mother, they would have been the ones to call us. Brandon had gone from foster home to foster home, and he seemed to know she was lying, too. That was one of the hardest things for me to see. Just thinking about it still makes my body freeze up today.

After the experience with Brandon and Tashira we started to only take care of babies, because they're innocent about the ways of the world. The babies who came through our house stayed from as little as one week to as long as three years. A social worker from the agency would call and say, "Hello, we have a baby." Then she would describe the child. My sister or I would tell my mother and she would say, "OK."

"OK," the social worker would say. She would verify our address and, as soon as they found us (most of the time they would get lost and call a couple of times before they finally found our apartment), they would come up to the fifth floor, knock on our door and leave us the child and whatever they had for him or her: clothes, baby formula, diapers, etc. They would answer a couple of questions about the child's name, who his mother was—if they knew—and what situation had caused the baby to be placed in foster care (like being abandoned or coming from a family that had drug or alcohol problems). Then they would leave.

Almost in the blink of an eye, "my little brother" became a stranger.

Every child who came to the house had a different story. And every story had to do with drugs. Sometimes their mothers were addicts who abandoned them in the hospital days after giving birth to them or just left them on the street. Many of the babies were born with drugs in their blood and would have seizures where they would start shaking all of a sudden. All except one had relatives who were fighting for custody in court at the time we had them.

I never got too attached to any of these kids. Until Joseph. Joseph came to us when he was 12 days old. His mother had left him in the hospital and no one knew or heard from any of his relatives. Everyone in my family got attached to him, especially me. I used to feed him and change his diapers sometimes. I would tickle him to make him laugh and play peek-a-boo with him. Since no one had ever claimed him, it was like he was ours.

After 11 months, we were planning to adopt Joseph—something we'd never contemplated doing with any other child. It was like he completed our family. Joseph was "my little brother." I got a pin-the-tail-on-the-donkey game for his first birthday which was coming up on April 20. "For Joseph's first birthday," I wrote on it so no one would try to take it.

Just when we were planning his birthday party and adoption, we got a phone call telling us that Joseph's aunt had decided to claim him and had gone to court and won custody.

The day before Joseph left I could hardly look at him. I remember he was in his walker and he came into my room and my sister pushed him out. I understood that he was just a child and wasn't at fault, but it was like a part of me was dying and he was there smiling and laughing just to torment me. It was all happening so fast and I was only 10 years old.

As soon as the paperwork went through, on March 22, Joseph was taken from us. His first night in his aunt's house, Joseph cried the whole night. He cried until he tired himself out and fell asleep and then he'd wake up and start crying again.

My brother and my father had to drive to Joseph's new house in another part of Brooklyn in the middle of the night to put him to sleep. He cried like that for about three weeks. Can you imagine being 11 months old and, in a split second, not knowing where you are or who you're with?

Almost in the blink of an eye, "my little brother" became a stranger. After they took him away, I felt like I could never love again. It was like my heart had been ripped out of my chest, thrown against a wall and then stepped on. This child I loved and cared for could someday walk by me in the street and not know that I once held him in my arms. He wouldn't know that I ever made him laugh. I still have that pin-the-tail-on-the-donkey game and it's never been opened.

More kids came and went after Joseph but I tried not to get too attached. I would still play with them and love them, but I would always remind myself that they would someday leave and I would never see them again. I also reminded myself that it wasn't their fault. The saddest thing for me was looking into all those children's eyes knowing what they're probably in for in this world.

Probably the saddest case I've seen was a baby that we had about two years ago, named David. His mother was 14 or 15 when she had him. She was addicted to drugs and went into rehabilitation so she could someday get her son back. My mother met her and David's grandmother when she took him to the agency and later described how the girl's mother badmouthed her in front of everyone there—calling her worthless and stupid. My mother was shocked and felt sorry for her because, she said, David's mother was just a child herself.

Less than a month after that, the agency called and when I got home from school my mother told me that David's mother ended up running away from the rehab to get high on drugs, and she overdosed and died. I just looked at David. My only thought was that he'd just been brought into this world and already he had lost his mother.

I've learned so many things about the world through my experiences with my foster brothers and sisters. Now, when I meet someone, I'm aware that you never know what he or she has been through in life or why people do the things they do. I always respect people and try to get to know them before I pass any judgments about them. Being a part of a foster family has also made me care more about people. Most people would say that was good, but sometimes I care too much.

I've seen these kids get lied to all the time and it hurts. It's made it hard for me to trust anybody. I also distance myself from people and look more on the negative aspects of things so that in the end I won't get hurt. My logic is that if I had never let myself think that Joseph was going to stay, I might not have felt so bad in the end when they took him away.

Over the years, we've heard from some of the kids' families by phone, and a couple of weeks ago, one of them was dropped off by his parents to visit for a day. That only happens once in a blue moon though and then we never hear from them again.

Sometimes it's been annoying having kids in the house all the time. My mother would fight with my sister and me when we all wanted to go somewhere and complain that she was always in the house taking care of the kids. I sometimes feel cheated and used, because people dump their babies and then when the babies are starting to walk and talk, all of a sudden the families want them back. At times it's gotten to the point where we tell my mother not to take any more kids, but it's hard to reject an innocent child.

> *If I had never let myself think that Joseph was going to stay, I might not have felt so bad in the end when they took him away.*

Now I don't really pay much attention to the kids unless they're crying (which annoys me). When I think of all the kids that have come in and out of my life and all the experiences that have come with them, I feel old. Still, I can't imagine what I would be like if I had never experienced this.

In addition to all the annoyances and learning about all the bad stuff in this world, I have learned a lesson in love. Even if it hurts knowing that you're never going to see the kids again once they're gone, knowing that you've been able to help makes it all worth it. They never asked to be born, none of us did. They deserve a fair chance in life too, and a foster family like ours can help provide that for a child.

Ana wrote this story when she was 18. She later graduated from New York University, went to business school, and worked in public relations.

Jamaal Pascall

Losing Another Family

By Tamecka Crawford

In June I was told that my group home in the Bronx, in New York City, would be closing down by the end of the summer due to budget cuts. A staff person from the agency called a meeting to tell us the news, though some of us had already heard rumors. He told us not to worry, that we would still be taken care of and moved to another group home. But at that point, it was still too early for him or anyone else to say where we would go.

When an agency makes the decision to close a group home, they are taking away people's homes and jobs, but I feel they may not realize the effect it has on us. Many residents have had to alter our lives many times because we've lost our families and homes—and when a group home closes, we're losing them all over again.

When I heard my group home was closing I was confused.

It appeared to me that the other residents were, too. Some of the girls, including me, started to cry. We couldn't understand why this was happening to us.

When you hear something as upsetting as this, your heart races as if it's the end of the world. You want to be told exactly what is going to happen to you, like where and when you are going to be moved, and whatever else pops into your mind.

I turned 21 years old in September and would have had to leave the group home anyway, but I was still hurt. This has been my home for two years. I have grown and matured here. Some of the staff members went beyond the call of duty to make that group home a home-like setting for us.

I had developed a close attachment to the residents and staff, which is very hard to do in the foster care system. It felt like my entire family was being split apart. I felt helpless. There wasn't anything we could do about it—our group home was closing regardless.

You want to be told exactly what is going to happen to you, like where and when you are going to be moved.

I interviewed residents and staff to find out how they felt when they were told the group home was closing.

At first it appeared to me as if the residents were suffering but the staff were dealing with it all right. But after I interviewed some staff members, I learned that they were hurting almost as much as the residents.

The three staff members I interviewed are: Ms. Barbara Montana, 41, a child-care worker who has worked with the agency for nine years; Ms. Sherry Best, 23, a social worker who has been with the agency for 10 months; and Mr. Eugene Hunter, 58, a supervisor who has worked with the agency for 17 years.

Tamecka: What was your first reaction to the closing of the group home?

Ms. Best: After I heard the house was closing in that manner I was really shocked.

Mr. Hunter: After my director told me...I was in a state of shock...You would never think that something like this could happen. This is a good program and the girls really benefited from this house.

Tamecka: What impact has the closing had on the residents?

Ms. Montana: We were a family and all of a sudden we were being torn apart. It felt as if nobody wanted [the residents] anymore, like they gave up on them.

Ms. Best: Many of the residents are frightened because they don't have any family to go home to. For some residents, this had been their home for many years. They are wondering where they are going to go. At this point the residents are reaching out to undesirables for protection, because they feel they won't have a place to live.

When my group home closed, it felt like my entire family was being split apart.

Mr. Hunter: The residents don't know what they are going to do. They're AWOL, getting angry with the staff; they are also working things out on their own.

Tamecka: How have you helped the residents deal with the closing of the group home?

Ms. Montana: It wasn't too much I could say, we were all walking around like zombies. We were all just shocked.

Ms. Best: Myself, the childcare workers, the manager, the supervisor, and the clinician (psychologist) are meeting with the residents and talking about their feelings surrounding the closing of the group home. In those meetings we discuss future plans, placements, and places they would like to be, and we also talk about alternatives. We ask the residents to think about what life would be like when the group home closes. There are tears, they fear they will endure more hardship. One person is not enough to help the residents; it's a team project.

Tamecka: What do you have to say to the residents who are

still in fear?

Ms. Best: I'll just let them know that it's not the end of the world, to move on and make the best out of what they have to work with. One thing they are not going to be is on the streets.

I also interviewed several residents of my former group home: Vanessa Agee, 16, who has been in foster care for 11 months; Betzaida Santana, 18, who has been in foster care for six years and in five group homes; Denise Archbold, 20, who has been in seven group homes since she was 12 years old; and Carlean Francois, 18, who has been in foster care for three years and in three different group homes.

Tamecka: How do you feel about moving again?

Vanessa: I don't like moving because this is my first group home and it's really nice.

Betzaida: I feel more hurt than anything because it's now that I'm getting myself together. I'm a senior in high school...I'm currently working ...and I'm also considered one of the elite girls of the agency and everything is going good for me.

Tamecka: What was your first reaction when you discovered your group home was closing?

Vanessa: Oh my God! I felt very bad, because I was thinking, where would we go? Would we have a place to live? And also how would we survive?

Denise: I was upset, I was crying, and also I was moody because I don't have a place to go.

Carlean: I was mad, I cried a little, and was thinking, "Where am I going to live?" I feel left in the cold and abandoned because I really can't handle being out on my own right now... because I don't know what to do.

Tamecka: What did you think would happen to you when the group home closes?

Denise: I thought and still feel a little that I'll be on the streets.

Tamecka: Has anyone helped you cope with the closing of the

group home?

Betzaida: [My] social worker. She sits down and talks to me and encourages me, but she really doesn't have much information.

Carlean: Yes, but they speak in general, not [about] what is going to happen to me.

Tamecka: Do you feel prepared to deal with the group home closing?

Vanessa: Yes, because I already got it in my mind that the house is closing and I know I have to find some place that's going to work out for me.

Denise: No, because I'm not financially prepared and I don't have a job.

Carlean: Yes and then no...I've been out on my own before, but I always had the group home to fall back on.

Tamecka: Any last comments?

Betzaida: I just hope all the girls end up somewhere that doesn't get them down because living in the system you can get brought down a lot.

Carlean: I am mostly concerned about the staff and what's going to happen to them. I may not show it but it's the staff that I really care for...They're like my parents.

So, as you can see, everyone is emotionally affected by this. After building up that togetherness, you don't want to pick up and move again where you may not get that same type of closeness.

On the day we first heard the news, while we were getting ready for bed, most of the girls were discussing their feelings of abandonment. Most were totally scared. Some thought they would be thrown out on the street, others that they would have to find an apartment or place to live. All of these fears are understandable when you've discovered your home is being taken away.

But if you or someone you know is in a group home that's

closing, there are some things you should know that might help you avoid the fear we felt: No matter when or how a group home closes, you will be taken care of until your 21st birthday. And, although you may want to know everything at once about where you'll be going, your agency may not tell you anything while they're working on new placements. All of this takes time, so while you may have been told that your group home is closing, things are still being worked out.

When an agency decides it must close a group home, it investigates various options for each resident. Those include: placement in another of the agency's group homes or foster homes; placement with another agency that has a similar program to fit the individual's needs; or returning to the family or another relative if possible.

As of now, all the girls from my group home were placed either in another group home within my agency, with family members, or in different agencies. Some of the staff moved to the agency's other group home and the rest were laid off.

Tamecka was 20 when she wrote this story.
She graduated high school and attended college.

YC Art Dept.

How Make Moving Easier on Teens

By Hattie Rice and Erica Harrigan

A few weeks ago we met with New York City's foster care administrators to talk about their policy of moving teens from group homes to foster homes. At the end of the meeting, one woman said to us, "You seem totally fed up with the system. What could we be doing differently?"

On the spot, we weren't sure what could have made the process easier. But later on, we tried to come up with some answers. Here they are:

1) Give us more time.

Close connections take a while to build. "The main problem with the permanency policy is the quickness. I don't think there should be a deadline on finding a permanent connection. An important decision like that can't be rushed. Getting told I'd need to move in two months made me feel like a case number instead of an individual." —Hattie

2) Explain your reasons for moving us to foster or adoptive homes.

"Take time explaining things like adoption to kids. When I was 12, my foster mother informed me that I was being adopted. I assumed she was trying to be my mother, and I felt I didn't need a mother. I already had one. When she told me, I got violent. I got sent to a mental institution. In the hospital, I wondered, 'If I were that woman's real child, would she have discarded me or given me another chance?' Now I wish I'd accepted my foster mom adopting me. In my teen years, I realized my adoptive parent wouldn't have been a replacement of my biological mother, but someone I could count on when I leave care." —Erica

> **Foster parents can't be so quick to throw us out.**

3) Get to know us before you move us.

"It feels horrible not to have a bond with the people who make decisions for me. How do they know what's best for me? They don't know. That feels like walking in a maze, blindfolded, and having to trust a stranger to find the door that opens my future." —Hattie

4) Train the foster parents to understand teens.

"I think it should be more difficult to become foster parents. Foster parents should have secure jobs so teens know the parents are looking for a child to love, not extra zeroes. They should also have degrees in psychology, or be good communicators, because you have to know how to talk. If foster parents have certain expectations of teens in their homes, they should explain that up front so the teen and foster parent are not disappointed. They should also ask teens what rules they're used to and compromise on what's going to be OK in their new home. Most of all, foster parents need to be trained to think of how they'd handle their kids in similar situations. Technically, we are their kids. They can't be so quick to throw us out." —Hattie

Teens need to learn how to express themselves, how to talk about what's bothering them.

5) Do mediation.

"Foster parents and the kids need help coming to an understanding about curfew, chores, punishments. In a new home, teens are going to act up. Sometimes they'll even be defiant, vindictive and hateful—and foster parents can be, too. We all have to deal with funky attitudes. I think a social worker needs to help the kids and parents work together to find out where the bad behavior is stemming from and solve the problem. Teens need to learn how to express themselves, how to talk about what's bothering them, so they can grow up to be successful adults who know how to handle situations correctly." —Erica

---

Hattie was 15 and Erica was 19 when they wrote this story.

Keysha Ramos

Am I Too Angry to Love?

By Aquellah Mahdi

This summer, ACS (New York City's foster care system) announced that it was closing the group home I've lived in for the past three years. I found out that my twin sister and I would have to move to a foster home.

Right before the house shut down, my sister and I visited a foster mother in the Bronx. She asked us, "What do you like to eat?"

I told her, "You'll get a list if we come to live with you."

Then she asked us to have something to drink and we agreed. She gave me a ginger drink that burned my mouth. I hated it. I text messaged my sister saying, "Don't drink it," but she did anyway and got a surprise.

Then came our small room. I didn't like it. After that, it was time to go. On the train, we told our social worker we hoped that we didn't have to live there. But a week later we moved in. I was angry, and a little fearful.

I would like foster parents who make me feel like I am a part of their lives, not an outsider or stranger, and who want me to be who I am and don't judge me on my past or what's in my file. But when I came into foster care four years ago, my sister and I lived with five different foster families in less than a year.

The worst was our fifth foster home. There I was sexually abused by the foster mother's best friend. That experience still haunts me. The foster mom ignored the abuse. I still wonder, "Where was she? Did she even care about me?" It's hard for me to imagine trusting another foster mom.

It was a relief when my sister and I got placed in our group home. The group home became our own little environment with rules that we made for ourselves. We cooked for ourselves, washed our clothes, and prepared for our future on the mean streets of the world.

I don't want any stranger to try to take control of the life that my sister and I have built for ourselves.

It felt good to be my own boss. I got to make the decisions in my life. I took the blame for anything that went wrong or that I didn't like. But it hurt not to have anyone looking out for me. When friends would talk about fights they had with their parents, or when their parents would show up for school events, I would just sit and watch all the parents. When I heard people say, "Twins are wonderful," I'd think to myself, "Someone out there has to want us."

When we moved in with that foster mom in the Bronx, I hoped she'd try to be there for us.

The first day she wasn't even there. I was angry and hurt. I guess that's because after I spoke up about the abuse and came into foster care, my mother and father wanted nothing to do with me. I began to believe that any adult who said they'd care for me would be just like them. I wanted to leave that night.

When the foster mom came home, she seemed to believe that my sister and I were little children who needed the world from her. She wanted me to call her "Mom" or "Aunt." I have a bad relationship with my mom and my aunt. I thought, "You want me to treat you like I treat them?" Then she cooked for us and we didn't eat what she cooked. We waited until she was done and cooked what we wanted.

I made a list of things my sister and I eat so she could buy our food, but she didn't buy exactly what we wanted. She bought the wrong kind of cereal, she put ginger in the juice even though I told her not to, and the bread was some damn thick Jamaican bread. So we bought our own food and she got mad.

She said, "I didn't really know what to buy."

"Then what the hell was the list for?" I said.

"I was looking and I didn't find what was on the list," she said.

"Well, I found it," I told her. She sucked her teeth and walked away.

All of these little things made me furious. I believed she thought it didn't matter what I told her, and that she could treat us how she wants. I don't want any stranger to try to take control of the life that my sister and I have built for ourselves. I'm afraid that if I give up control—even over what I eat—then I will feel like I did when my dad was sexually abusing me: Like a doll in someone else's playhouse being used for everything that person desires.

Our first weekend there, we went AWOL. My foster mother kept calling me on my cell. When we came home she told me, "I was worried."

I said, "I do have a sister who came along with me. Why do

you keep addressing all of the problems to me?" Then she got mad.

It seemed like one minute she wanted to be my best friend and worry about me, the next she got angry, showing her dark side. When foster mothers switch like that, I'm reminded of my mom. One minute she was nice; then she would get so mean and hard to handle. My mother abused me even more emotionally than physically. I'm afraid a foster mom will, too.

Whenever I feel threatened I get this feeling that I want to hurt anybody who might try to harm me and my sister. So I started cursing at the foster mom. I wanted her to lose control. I figured that sooner or later she would say something that would hurt me. I wanted to hurt her first.

When my emotions came out, she got to feel the hurt from my past. When she closed the door and I called her one last name, I won and she lost. Yelling at her made me feel powerful. I knew that no matter how much she might scare me or worry me, I could still get the last word or the upper hand.

Later I felt depressed. I knew I'd acted out of control. When I get angry I don't even realize what I do and I hurt the people around me. When I think of all the people I've hurt because of my anger I feel bad. This pattern of abuse that I've inherited from my parents is one I want to break. But I don't know how.

After two weeks, the foster mom told my social worker that she wanted us out. She told my sister and me that we could never be a part of her family because we don't listen. That hurt me. I didn't want to live with her, but I didn't want her to reject me, either.

That day, I wished I could be on my own. I thought I'd feel better about myself if I didn't have anyone telling me what to do. But I also felt afraid of having no one to look over me. What if I'm not stable enough to cope out in the real world? What if my anger gets the best of me? Who will I turn to?

I hope that foster mother understood all of my troubles with foster homes, my past and my feelings toward myself. I fear myself sometimes. I'm afraid that I may become like my mother—mean and out of control.

I feel sad that I'm not good about expressing myself. I feel like a walking time bomb. I hope I can find a foster mom who can handle my anger, and help me take control of myself.

The writer was 18 when she wrote this story. She later found a supportive foster mother and attended Lehman College.

YC Art Dept.

Keeping My Bags Packed

By Taheerah Mahdi

When my twin sister Aquellah and I moved to a group home three years ago, I assumed we'd stay there until we turned 18 and then move to an apartment program. Then one night a staff said to me, "This place is closing."

I hoped she was joking, so I asked, "How do you know?"

She pointed to the bedrooms. "Look, Taheerah. Who came home last night, huh? The night before? Only three girls are here. She told me the house would close in two months.

Later, my social worker explained that the group home was closing because city foster care officials believe that teens like me would be better off in foster homes.

I worried, "What will happen to us if we move to a foster home?" I had reason to believe that a foster home wouldn't work out. Before we got to the group home, Aquellah and I had lived in six different foster homes. It was crazy. I never felt settled. I was always on the move. After the first few homes I wondered, "Why should I try to get to know these people? I might as well keep my bags packed, because I'll be moving again."

A week after I learned my home was closing, some social workers came and asked us each if we knew anyone we'd like to live with. I thought I knew someone. She was a staff at my group home whom I'd known for about four months. My sister and I had gotten attached to her quickly. We fit together like a puzzle because we'd all been through the same things.

I began to wonder, "Will anyone want us?"

She asked us to live with her and we said yes. But she was always out smoking or drinking, sometimes with my sister and me. When she got drunk she would cry and say, "I'm sorry, do you still want to live with me?"

After a while, I started to hate her. I hated that she got high, I hated when she would cry. Her dependency on me reminded me of my mom. I felt like I had my old position back: I was the adult, in charge of her. My dreams of a normal life vanished when I saw that her desire to drink and get high was deeper than her desire to take us.

After that fell apart, I didn't know anyone else who would take me. My godmother is the closest adult in my life, but she's told me that she doesn't have space for my sister and me.

My social worker said she would look for a therapeutic foster home for us. I thought "therapeutic" meant that I was crazy and needed therapy all day and all night. I felt like she was saying I couldn't take care of myself, or that I'd never be able to live on my own. The label hurt.

As other girls found homes, the house got quiet. I began to wonder, "Will anyone want us?"

Then I met Crystal. Crystal was taking my friend Raquel to

live with her. As my sister and I helped Raquel with her stuff I was crying because Raquel was leaving and nobody had called to take me.

Crystal noticed and said, "Oooo, twins! I love twins." Later she called and asked if we wanted to spend the weekend. We packed our bags. She said, "Come on, twins, let's go." We got in the car and rode off.

We got to her house late Friday night. She has a big house, with stairs up to the front door and a little dog that barks like she's big. Crystal said, "Eat your ice cream and get to bed. I'll see ya in the morning."

When she left the room, Raquel said, "She wants you two to come here." I was happy and confused. I ate my ice cream. Then my sister and I went to the sun room and fell asleep on the couch.

We visited Crystal three times. I loved being with her. She was always driving somewhere and I would stick my head out the window and act like I was flying. Then Crystal would say, "Don't lean out the window." I would look out and daydream.

By the time our social worker called to say we could meet another foster mom, I felt so angry I didn't want to meet anyone else.

I felt comfortable because Crystal put our feelings first. Usually when I meet people and tell them about being in a group home, they want to know how I got there and ask questions leading to my past. Not once did she ask to know anything about our past. Her house felt so accepting. Each person was different but we all seemed to fit under the same roof, like a normal family.

But Crystal's home wasn't "therapeutic," so my social worker arranged for us to meet a different foster mom the week before our group home closed.

This foster mom was short, fat, and looked like an old foster mother whose boyfriend tried to molest my sister and me. She said that she had rules for us to follow, like she wanted us to clean everyone's dishes and come in at 10.

I couldn't understand how my judge and ACS would send us to a place where we had to live by stricter rules, and I got angry. I was about to turn 18 and had gotten used to independence in the group home, where I could go out whenever I wanted. Things went badly as soon as we moved in, partly because I judged the foster mom before I got to know her.

After a few days, we ran out of the building and went to stay with our friend Kimmy. That night, we stayed up like warriors and drank alcohol, wearing our bras and underwear, talking about the past and our group home. We ended up staying with Kimmy for four days.

When our social worker called Aquellah's cell phone and said we would be reported "missing" to the police, I didn't care. I told myself, "I am a runaway, unwanted by the city and crazy."

When the weekend ended we returned to the foster home. Going back made me want to scream. By the time our social worker called a week later to say we could meet another foster mom, I felt so angry I didn't want to meet anyone else. At the meeting, I knew I had to be on my best behavior. But I lost control.

We met Ms. Jones in a McDonald's. She told us that she was in foster care when she was younger. Then we talked about living with her. She also had rules, mainly a curfew, which we said we wouldn't follow.

"Why are you so angry?" she asked me because I was staring at her with an angry look on my face.

I told her, "Because I'm tired of getting sent around like I'm a piece of crap."

She said she understood how we felt. I thought, "The fact is, you don't. Just because you were in care doesn't mean you understand me."

Aquellah and I both had an attitude that caused tension in the air. And we would not stop cursing. Ms. Jones tried to be calm and ask what I thought of her neighborhood. I told her, "I think your neighborhood is a piece of @#%*."

"I'm not afraid of you two," she said.

"Good. That means that you don't just follow what they say about us," I said.

She ended the interview by saying we needed to fix our attitudes. When she left, I relaxed by breathing slowly. Then I told my social worker, "I feel like garbage." I felt depressed and frustrated with myself. I've been trying to practice self-control, but since we left the group home, my emotions have been getting the best of me.

A few days ago ACS moved us to another foster home. The woman seems mad nice. Our first night there, Aquellah was holding her baby bunny when the bunny jumped off her shoulder and, when she hit the floor, stopped breathing. Aquellah tried to do CPR on the bunny, but she was dead.

Aquellah began to cry, and so did the foster mom. She even gave Aquellah a hug.

That weekend was our birthday. We went to Crystal's for the day, but when we came back, our new foster mother baked us a cake that tasted so good. She told us that her family had watched lots of scary movies on TV the night before. I wished I'd been home with them.

Getting my hopes up, getting let down, and moving all around has been really stressful. I don't know this foster mom yet, but I hope I'll finally be able to put my head down and call her place my home.

Taheerah was 18 when she wrote this story.
She later attended college.

Take It Slow: How to Get to Know a New Family

Cori Herzig, a therapist in Santa Rosa, California, explains some good techniques for adjusting to a new family—and how you know when it's just not working out.

Q: How can you get to know a new foster family?

A: A major part of adjusting to a family is learning their routine. Not just how they wash the dishes or when they eat, but how open they are and what's OK to say around them. Learn when you can be more relaxed and what are signs you should keep your mouth shut. You know with your own family: "When dad comes in with that look on his face, I'm not going to bring up that I need money." Or, "When mom is stirring her coffee a certain way, she's stressed."

Noticing when is a good time to talk and when isn't will help you get the response you want when you open up. If you open up at the wrong moment, you risk a feeling of rejection which can snowball into feeling misunderstood.

You can also remember that it's a typical thing for teens to feel misunderstood by their families. Teens have so much going on inside, and all teens wonder, "What's my place?" Add to that having to adjust to a foster home, and it's going to be hard to figure out what's what.

Q: How do know if you're trusting too much or not enough?

A: When I was young, my mother became a foster parent to teenage girls. Some would come in and call her "mom" immediately and tell their life story to everyone in the household. Other girls that had been burned in their last placement or family of origin weren't going to tell anybody anything. If you're at one of those extremes, it's going to be harder for you to get close to people.

If you're opening up too quickly, you might feel overexposed or vulnerable, or you might be overwhelming others. Paying attention to your own body signals, in particular your breathing, can help. If you're talking really fast and breathing shallow, you might be talking out of fear, not a desire to be known. You can always slow down, breathe and trust yourself to go at a slower pace.

On the other end, if you hear people telling you, "It's hard to get to know you," or you feel apart from the family, you might want to try opening up more. The desire to be known is a healthy one.

Q: What are some signs that this isn't a good placement for you?

A: There are some obvious signs, like somebody is being verbally or physically abusive, or neglectful. Those are clearly not OK.

If you are making efforts to get to know people and you keep trying to communicate and work on it, and you keep feeling criticized or like you're in a hole and feeling like, "No matter what I do I can't get these people to like me," I don't think you should stay in that situation. Talk to social worker and say, "I've been trying." Tell the social worker everything you've tried, and say, "This isn't working. This feels bad for me."

But sometimes kids move from home to home because they come into a home almost daring the family to reject them, saying, "I don't have to adapt to you for me to belong. It's not fair." That anger is understandable, but if it becomes a central part of your identity that you won't adapt and you must be heard, it's going to be painful for you to try to connect to people even after you're out of foster care.

Julieth Riano / Dante Gutierrez

Building Trust, Brick by Brick

By Manny S.

By the time I got sent to my third foster home when I was 8 years old, I'd started to believe that all my experiences in foster care would be negative. I was trapped in a circle of revolving doors, and I didn't think I'd ever be able to stay in one place.

At my first foster home, there was a kid named Robert who thought he could bully my younger brother Daniel. One day I got so fed up with him that I punched him in the face, and my brother and I got kicked out. Then we were sent to live with my uncle, which was great, until he kicked us out. He said it was because Daniel and I were always fighting.

After getting the boot from my own family, I started to think I couldn't rely on them as much. I figured I could only be independent. I also believed that since I wasn't in those two homes for very long, my next home would be the same.

On my way to my next foster home I thought I'd better be ready to leave in three or four months, and I was already worried about where I'd get sent next. I was also scared of what my new foster mom would be like. I pictured her as a witch with razor-sharp teeth and claws.

I walked to the door with Daniel and my social worker and rang the bell. I heard barking and I was terrified at what she might have in that house—perhaps a pit bull trained to scare little kids, or torture them as they slept.

The door opened and I saw a woman with a happy face, anxious but full of excitement. She welcomed us in, but I was cautious due to what I'd heard at the door. Then I looked down, and saw a little dog whose bark was way bigger than his bite.

I looked around the apartment and I liked what I saw, but I was still on my toes.

The woman said her name was Melba. She showed us our room and told us to make ourselves at home, but I didn't unpack my things just yet. I felt like there was no point since we would be leaving soon anyway. My brother and I stood in the hall as Melba and my social worker talked in the living room. I started to imagine the horrible things she would do or make us do when my social worker left.

Since I wasn't in my first two foster homes for very long, I figured my next home would be the same.

When my social worker came in to say goodbye I thought, "Yup, this is it." I heard the door slam shut and my heart started to pound as I heard footsteps closing in toward the room, but I played it cool and sat on the bed. Her mouth opened and just when I thought she was going to breathe fire, she asked, "Are you guys hungry?"

Daniel said yes, but I said no. I was, but I wasn't comfortable asking her for anything. When she went to use the bathroom, I ran to the kitchen and grabbed a little something to eat.

The first few months were all the same. I would get home

from school, go to my room, close the door and do my homework. When Melba would come by and ask if I was hungry I'd usually say no. She didn't annoy me or force me to eat. She gave me my space, which was what I wanted. At dinnertime, I would just stay in my room.

Most of the time when I was in my bedroom, Melba would come in and ask if I'd finished doing my homework. I have to admit, it felt good to know she cared. We'd sometimes have little awkward encounters. Maybe a "Hey" or "Hi" but nothing more than that.

After five or six months, I started thinking I might be here longer than I'd thought. I also noticed Melba's consistency when it came to feeding me and checking my homework. Sometimes I'd take some change off her dresser to see how she'd react, but she never seemed frustrated.

I started to feel a little warmer inside. I began to answer, "Yes," when she asked if I was hungry, and I started leaving the door to my bedroom open. We even started to have conversations about things we liked or had in common. I found out that she'd had other foster children living there, but they were given back to their families. I thought that maybe the same thing would happen to me.

I felt happy that under Melba's care those kids had "survived" long enough to be returned to their families. I felt she could do the same for me until I was reunited with my family. This let me feel comfortable trusting Melba. Pretty soon I started to hug her when I came home from school, and I started showing her more affection than any of my previous foster moms.

On my 9th birthday, Melba took Daniel and me to the World Trade Center, which I'd never visited. When we got to a huge building that towered over me, she said, "We're here." I thought that we were going to do something boring, but I was shocked when we got inside. There was actually a huge variety of shores and restaurants. I'd never seen anything like it in my entire life.

We looked everywhere and we got to eat pizza at a cool restaurant, which I wasn't used to. When we sat down I tried to think of the last time I'd eaten at a table like that. I was so happy that she remembered my birthday, took me somewhere and had gotten me a present.

After that, I opened up a lot more. I believed that Melba had paid her dues and earned her stripes as my foster mom. I started talking to Melba a lot, and I often found myself the one starting the conversations. We'd talk about the news, school, TV and anything else worth talking about. The conversations weren't three hours long, but they were progress nonetheless. I also began to get closer to her family, which was cool. They didn't live with us, but they all treated me as if I was really part of their family.

Around the time I turned 14, I realized adoption was a possibility. We didn't really talk about it, but as time went on I knew that eventually it had to happen.

One day Melba sat me on the couch and said, "If you want to be adopted, I am here for you." I had grown to love

I noticed Melba's consistency when it came to feeding me and checking my homework.

Melba, but the idea that I couldn't live with my parents again seemed weird to me, and made me sad. I had to think about my situation before I could make a decision.

For years, my birth mother had filled my head with the dream that I'd be going home. But it never happened. Every time she made a promise that I could go home and then didn't keep it, I felt knocked down to the ground. That's when my mother would come again and lift up me up, only to knock me down again. But eventually, I got used to her routine.

When I finally realized that going back home wasn't going to happen, I knew that adoption was what I wanted. Now we're in the process of making that happen.

Melba has already been my parent for so long; the only thing that the adoption will change is that my brother and I will legally belong to her. Melba has given me advice and taught me those life lessons that you need to succeed, like saving money, helping people and taking school seriously.

Melba and I have developed a bond over the past several years. I am happy that I finally got a break from the negativity, and soon it will be permanent. Melba has been my salvation from a dramatic and awful life. We started from one brick and built a skyscraper of trust, understanding and love.

Manny was 15 when he wrote this story.

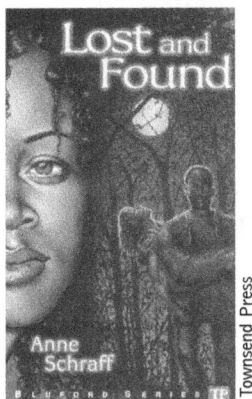

Townsend Press

Lost and Found

Darcy Wills winced at the loud rap music coming from her sister's room.

My rhymes were rockin'
MC's were droppin'
People shoutin' and hip-hoppin'
Step to me and you'll be inferior
'Cause I'm your lyrical superior.

Darcy went to Grandma's room. The darkened room smelled of lilac perfume, Grandma's favorite, but since her stroke Grandma did not notice it, or much of anything.

"Bye, Grandma," Darcy whispered from the doorway. "I'm going to school now."

Just then, the music from Jamee's room cut off, and Jamee rushed into the hallway.

The teen characters in the Bluford novels, a fiction series by Townsend Press, struggle with many of the same difficult issues as the writers in this book. Here's the first chapter from *Lost and Found*, by Anne Schraff, the first book in the series. In this novel, high school sophomore Darcy contends with the return of her long-absent father, the troubling behavior of her younger sister Jamee, and the beginning of her first relationship.

"Like she even hears you," Jamee said as she passed Darcy. Just two years younger than Darcy, Jamee was in eighth grade, though she looked older.

"It's still nice to talk to her. Sometimes she understands. You want to pretend she's not here or something?"

"She's not," Jamee said, grabbing her backpack.

"Did you study for your math test?" Darcy asked. Mom was an emergency room nurse who worked rotating shifts. Most of the time, Mom was too tired to pay much attention to the girls' schoolwork. So Darcy tried to keep track of Jamee.

"Mind your own business," Jamee snapped.

"You got two D's on your last report card," Darcy scolded. "You wanna flunk?" Darcy did not want to sound like a nagging parent, but Jamee wasn't doing her best. Maybe she couldn't make A's like Darcy, but she could do better.

Jamee stomped out of the apartment, slamming the door behind her. "Mom's trying to get some rest!" Darcy yelled. "Do you have to be so selfish?" But Jamee was already gone, and the apartment was suddenly quiet.

Darcy loved her sister. Once, they had been good friends. But now all Jamee cared about was her new group of rowdy friends. They leaned on cars outside of school and turned up rap music on their boom boxes until the street seemed to tremble like an earthquake. Jamee had even stopped hanging out with her old friend Alisha Wrobel, something she used to do every weekend.

Darcy went back into the living room, where her mother sat in the recliner sipping coffee. "I'll be home at 2:30, Mom," Darcy said. Mom smiled faintly. She was tired, always tired. And lately she was worried too. The hospital where she worked was cutting staff. It seemed each day fewer people were expected to do more work. It was like trying to climb a mountain that keeps getting taller as you go. Mom was forty-four, but just yesterday she said, "I'm like an old car that's run out of warranty, baby. You know what happens then. Old car is ready for the junk heap. Well, maybe that hospital is gonna tell me one of these days—'Mattie Mae Wills, we don't need you anymore. We can get somebody younger and cheaper.'"

"Mom, you're not old at all," Darcy had said, but they were only words, empty words. They could not erase the dark, weary lines from beneath her mother's eyes.

Darcy headed down the street toward Bluford High School. It was not a terrible neighborhood they lived in; it just was not good. Many front yards were not cared for. Debris—fast food wrappers, plastic bags, old newspapers—blew around and piled against fences and curbs. Darcy hated that. Sometimes she and other kids from school spent Saturday mornings cleaning up, but it seemed a losing battle. Now, as she walked, she tried to focus on small spots of beauty along the way. Mrs. Walker's pink and white roses bobbed proudly in the morning breeze. The Hustons' rock garden was carefully designed around a wooden windmill.

As she neared Bluford, Darcy thought about the science project that her biology teacher, Ms. Reed, was assigning. Darcy was doing hers on tidal pools. She was looking forward to visiting a real tidal pool, taking pictures, and doing research. Today, Ms. Reed would be dividing the students into teams of two. Darcy wanted to be paired with her close friend, Brisana Meeks. They were both excellent students, a cut above most kids at Bluford, Darcy thought.

"Today, we are forming project teams so that each student can gain something valuable from the other," Ms. Reed said as Darcy sat at her desk. Ms. Reed was a tall, stately woman who reminded Darcy of the Statue of Liberty. She would have been a perfect model for the statue if Lady Liberty had been a black woman. She never would have been called pretty, but it was possible she might have been called a handsome woman. "For this assignment, each of you will be working with someone you've never worked with before."

Darcy was worried. If she was not teamed with Brisana,

maybe she would be teamed with some really dumb student who would pull her down. Darcy was a little ashamed of herself for thinking that way. Grandma used to say that all flowers are equal, but different. The simple daisy was just as lovely as the prize rose. But still Darcy did not want to be paired with some weak partner who would lower her grade.

"Darcy Wills will be teamed with Tarah Carson," Ms. Reed announced.

Darcy gasped. Not Tarah! Not that big, chunky girl with the brassy voice who squeezed herself into tight skirts and wore lime green or hot pink satin tops and cheap jewelry. Not Tarah who hung out with Cooper Hodden, that loser who was barely hanging on to his football eligibility. Darcy had heard that Cooper had been left back once or twice and even got his driver's license as a sophomore. Darcy's face felt hot with anger. Why was Ms. Reed doing this?

Hakeem Randall, a handsome, shy boy who sat in the back row, was teamed with the class blabbermouth, LaShawn Appleby. Darcy had a secret crush on Hakeem since freshman year. So far she had only shared this with her diary, never with another living soul.

It was almost as though Ms. Reed was playing some devilish game. Darcy glanced at Tarah, who was smiling broadly. Tarah had an enormous smile, and her teeth contrasted harshly with her dark red lipstick. "Great," Darcy muttered under her breath.

Ms. Reed ord e red the teams to meet so they could begin to plan their projects.

As she sat down by Tarah, Darcy was instantly sickened by a syrupy-sweet odor.

She must have doused herself with cheap perfume this morning , Darcy thought.

"Hey, girl," Tarah said. "Well, don't you look down in the mouth. What's got you lookin' that way?"

It was hard for Darcy to meet new people, especially someone like Tarah, a person Aunt Charlotte would call "low class." These were people who were loud and rude. They drank too much, used drugs, got into fights and ruined the neighborhood. They yelled ugly insults at people, even at their friends. Darcy did not actually know that Tarah did anything like this personally, but she seemed like the type who did.

"I just didn't think you'd be interested in tidal pools," Darcy explained.

Tarah slammed her big hand on the desk, making her gold bracelets jangle like ice cubes in a glass, and laughed. Darcy had never heard a mule bray, but she was sure it made exactly the same sound. Then Tarah leaned close and whispered, "Girl, I don't know a tidal pool from a fool. Ms. Reed stuck us together to mess with our heads, you hear what I'm sayin'?"

"Maybe we could switch to other partners," Darcy said nervously.

A big smile spread slowly over Tarah's face. "Nah, I think I'm gonna enjoy this. You're always sittin' here like a princess collecting your A's. Now you gotta work with a regular person, so you better loosen up, girl!"

Darcy felt as if her teeth were glued to her tongue. She fumbled in her bag for her outline of the project. It all seemed like a horrible joke now. She and Tarah Carson standing knee-deep in the muck of a tidal pool!

"Worms live there, don't they?" Tarah asked, twisting a big gold ring on her chubby finger.

"Yeah, I guess," Darcy replied.

"Big green worms," Tarah continued. "So if you get your feet stuck in the bottom of that old tidal pool, and you can't get out, do the worms crawl up your clothes?"

Darcy ignored the remark. "I'd like for us to go there soon, you know, look around."

"My boyfriend, Cooper, he goes down to the ocean all the time. He can take us. He says he's seen these fiddler crabs. They look like big spiders, and they'll try to bite your toes off. Cooper says so," Tarah said.

"Stop being silly," Darcy shot back. "If you're not even going to be serious . . . "

"You think you're better than me, don't you?" Tarah suddenly growled.

"I never said—" Darcy blurted.

"You don't have to say it, girl. It's in your eyes. You think I'm a low-life and you're something special. Well, I got more friends than you got fingers and toes together. You got no friends, and everybody laughs at you behind your back. Know what the word on you is? Darcy Wills give you the chills."

Just then, the bell rang, and Darcy was glad for the excuse to turn away from Tarah, to hide the hot tears welling in her eyes. She quickly rushed from the classroom, relieved that school was over. Darcy did not think she could bear to sit through another class just now.

Darcy headed down the long street towards home. She did not like Tarah. Maybe it was wrong, but it was true. Still, Tarah's brutal words hurt. Even stupid, awful people might tell you the truth about yourself. And Darcy did not have any real friends, except for Brisana. Maybe the other kids were mocking her behind her back. Darcy was very slender, not as shapely as many of the other girls. She remembered the time when Cooper Hodden was hanging in front of the deli with his friends, and he yelled as Darcy went by, "Hey, is that really a female there? Sure don't look like it. Looks more like an old broomstick with hair. " His companions laughed rudely, and Darcy had walked a little faster.

A terrible thought clawed at Darcy. Maybe she was the loser, not Tarah. Tarah was always hanging with a bunch of kids, laughing and joking. She would go down the hall to the lockers and greetings would come from everywhere. "Hey, Tarah!" "What's up, Tar?" "See ya at lunch, girl." When Darcy went to the lockers, there was dead silence.

Darcy usually glanced into stores on her way home from school. She enjoyed looking at the trays of chicken feet and pork ears at the little Asian grocery store. Sometimes she would even steal a glance at the diners sitting by the picture window at the Golden Grill Restaurant. But today she stared straight ahead, her shoulders drooping.

If this had happened last year, she would have gone directly to Grandma's house, a block from where Darcy lived. How many times had Darcy and Jamee run to Grandma's, eaten applesauce cookies, drunk cider, and poured out their troubles to Grandma. Somehow, their problems would always dissolve in the warmth of her love and wisdom. But now Grandma was a frail figure in the corner of their apartment, saying little. And what little she did say made less and less sense.

Darcy was usually the first one home. The minute she got there, Mom left for the hospital to take the 3:00 to 11:00 shift in the ER. By the time Mom finished her paperwork at the hospital, she would be lucky to be home again by midnight. After Mom left, Darcy went to Grandma's room to give her the malted nutrition drink that the doctor ordered her to have three times a day.

"Want to drink your chocolate malt, Grandma?" Darcy asked, pulling up a chair beside Grandma's bed.

Grandma was sitting up, and her eyes were open. "No. I'm not hungry," she said listlessly. She always said that.

"You need to drink your malt, Grandma," Darcy insisted, gently putting the straw between the pinched lips.

Grandma sucked the malt slowly. "Grandma, nobody likes me at school," Darcy said. She did not expect any response. But there was a strange comfort in telling Grandma anyway. "Everybody laughs at me. It's because I'm shy and maybe stuck-up, too, I guess. But I don't mean to be. Stuck-up, I mean. Maybe I'm weird. I could be weird, I guess. I could be like Aunt Charlotte . . ." Tears rolled down Darcy's cheeks. Her heart ached with loneliness. There was nobody to talk to anymore, nobody who had time to listen, nobody who understood.

Grandma blinked and pushed the straw away. Her eyes brightened as they did now and then. "You are a wonderful girl. Everybody knows that," Grandma said in an almost normal voice. It happened like that sometimes. It was like being in the middle of a dark storm and having the clouds part, revealing a patch of clear, sunlit blue. For just a few precious minutes, Grandma was bright-eyed and saying normal things.

"Oh, Grandma, I'm so lonely," Darcy cried, pressing her head against Grandma's small shoulder.

"You were such a beautiful baby," Grandma said, stroking her hair." 'That one is going to shine like the morning star.' That's what I told your Mama. 'That child is going to shine like the morning star.' Tell me, Angelcake, is your daddy home yet?"

Darcy straightened. "Not yet." Her heart pounded so hard, she could feel it thumping in her chest. Darcy's father had not been home in five years.

"Well, tell him to see me when he gets home. I want him to buy you that blue dress you liked in the store window. That's for you, Angelcake. Tell him I've got money. My social security came, you know. I have money for the blue dress," Grandma said, her eyes slipping shut.

Just then, Darcy heard the apartment door slam. Jamee had come home. Now she stood in the hall, her hands belligerently on her hips. "Are you talking to Grandma again?" Jamee demanded.

"She was talking like normal," Darcy said. "Sometimes she does. You know she does."

"That is so stupid," Jamee snapped. "She never says anything right anymore. Not anything!" Jamee's voice trembled.

Darcy got up quickly and set down the can of malted milk. She ran to Jamee and put her arms around her sister. "Jamee, I know you're hurting too."

"Oh, don't be stupid," Jamee protested, but Darcy hugged her more tightly, and in a few seconds Jamee was crying. "She was the best thing in this stupid house," Jamee cried. "Why'd she have to go?"

"She didn't go," Darcy said. "Not really."

"She did! She did!" Jamee sobbed. She struggled free of Darcy, ran to her room, and slammed the door. In a minute, Darcy heard the bone-rattling sound of rap music.

Lost and Found, a Bluford Series™ novel, is reprinted with permission from Townsend Press. Copyright © 2002.

Want to read more? This and other Bluford Series™ novels and paperbacks can be purchased for $1 each at www.townsendpress.com.

Teens:
How to Get More Out of This Book

Self-help: The teens who wrote the stories in this book did so because they hope that telling their stories will help readers who are facing similar challenges. They want you to know that you are not alone, and that taking specific steps can help you manage or overcome very difficult situations. They've done their best to be clear about the actions that worked for them so you can see if they'll work for you.

Writing: You can also use the book to improve your writing skills. Each teen in this book wrote 5-10 drafts of his or her story before it was published. If you read the stories closely you'll see that the teens work to include a beginning, a middle, and an end, and good scenes, description, dialogue, and anecdotes (little stories). To improve your writing, take a look at how these writers construct their stories. Try some of their techniques in your own writing.

Reading: Finally, you'll notice that we include the first chapter from a Bluford Series novel in this book, alongside the true stories by teens. We hope you'll like it enough to continue reading. The more you read, the more you'll strengthen your reading skills. Teens at Youth Communication like the Bluford novels because they explore themes similar to those in their own stories. Your school may already have the Bluford books. If not, you can order them online for only $1.

Resources on the Web

We will occasionally post Think About It questions on our website, www.youthcomm.org, to accompany stories in this and other Youth Communication books. We try out the questions with teens and post the ones they like best. Many teens report that writing answers to those questions in a journal is very helpful.

How to Use This Book in Staff Training

Staff say that reading these stories gives them greater insight into what teens are thinking and feeling, and new strategies for working with them. You can help the staff you work with by using these stories as case studies.

Select one story to read in the group, and ask staff to identify and discuss the main issue facing the teen. There may be disagreement about this, based on the background and experience of staff. That is fine. One point of the exercise is that teens have complex lives and needs. Adults can probably be more effective if they don't focus too narrowly and can see several dimensions of their clients.

Ask staff: What issues or feelings does the story provoke in them? What kind of help do they think the teen wants? What interventions are likely to be most promising? Least effective? Why? How would you build trust with the teen writer? How have other adults failed the teen, and how might that affect his or her willingness to accept help? What other resources would be helpful to this teen, such as peer support, a mentor, counseling, family therapy, etc.

Resources on the Web

From time to time we will post Think About It questions on our website, www.youthcomm.org, to accompany stories in this and other Youth Communication books. We try out the questions with teens and post the ones that they find most effective. We'll also post lesson for some of the stories. Adults can use the questions and lessons in workshops.

| Discussion Guide |

Teachers and Staff:
How to Use This Book in Groups

When working with teens individually or in groups, using these stories can help young people face difficult issues in a way that feels safe to them. That's because talking about the issues in the stories usually feels safer to teens than talking about those same issues in their own lives. Addressing issues through the stories allows for some personal distance; they hit close to home, but not too close. Talking about them opens up a safe place for reflection. As teens gain confidence talking about the issues in the stories, they usually become more comfortable talking about those issues in their own lives.

Below are general questions that can help you lead discussions about the stories, which help teens and staff reflect on the issues in their own work and lives. In most cases you can read a story and conduct a discussion in one 45-minute session. Teens are usually happy to read the stories aloud, with each teen reading a paragraph or two. (Allow teens to pass if they don't want to read.) It takes 10-15 minutes to read a story straight through. However, it is often more effective to let workshop participants make comments and discuss the story as you go along. The workshop leader may even want to annotate her copy of the story beforehand with key questions.

If teens read the story ahead of time or silently, it's good to break the ice with a few questions that get everyone on the same page: Who is the main character? How old is she? What happened to her? How did she respond? Etc. Another good starting question is: "What stood out for you in the story?" Go around the room and let each person briefly mention one thing.

Then move on to open-ended questions, which encourage participants to think more deeply about what the writers were feeling, the choices they faced, and they actions they took. There are no right or wrong answers to the open-ended questions. Open-ended questions encourage participants to think about how the themes, emotions and choices in the stories relate to their own lives. Here are some examples of open-ended questions that we have found to be effective. You can use variations of these questions with almost any story in this book.

—What main problem or challenge did the writer face?

—What choices did the teen have in trying to deal with the problem?

—Which way of dealing with the problem was most effective for the teen? Why?

—What strengths, skills, or resources did the teen use to address the challenge?

—If you were in the writer's shoes, what would you have done?

—What could adults have done better to help this young person?

—What have you learned by reading this story that you didn't know before?

—What, if anything, will you do differently after reading this story?

—What surprised you in this story?

—Do you have a different view of this issue, or see a different way of dealing with it, after reading this story? Why or why not?

Credits

The stories in this book originally appeared in the following Youth Communication publications:

"The Moving Game," by Quantwilla Johnson, *Represent*, January/February 1997

"Gotta Leave Again," by Forever Broughton, *Represent*, November/December 1999

"Looking for One Good Home," by Hattie Rice, *Represent*, November/December 2004

"Mail-Order Children," by Baudilio Lozado, *Represent*, September/October 1997

"Too Many Schools," by Akeema Lottman, *Represent*, March/April 2009

"Getting the Education You Deserve," by Akeema Lottman, *Represent*, March/April 2009

"Hard to Say Goodbye," by Sherelle Leggett, *New Youth Connections*, July/August 2008

"Torn Apart," by Anonymous, *Represent*, January/February 2009

"Keep Me in Da Hood," by Sylinda Sinkfield, *Represent*, September/October 1998

"Goodbye, Harlem," by Antwaun Garcia, *Represent*, March/April 2006

"My Life on the Move (Again)," by Sharif Berkeley, *Represent*, May/June 1995

"A Love Too Strong," by Tamecka Crawford, *Represent*, July/August 1994

"Fifteen Months in Care: And Fifteen Placements!" by Youniqiue Symone, *Represent*, May/June 1996

"Taken From the Home I Loved," by Charlene Johnson, *Represent*, September/October 1996

"My Foster Siblings: They Come and They Go," by Ana Angelica Pines, *New Youth Connections*, March 1997

"Losing Another Family," by Tamecka Crawford, *Represent*, September/October 1995

"Am I Too Angry to Love?" by Aquellah Mahdi, *Represent*, November/December 2004

"Keeping My Bags Packed," by Taheerah Mahdi, *Represent*, November/December 2004

"Take It Slow: How to get to know a new family," *Represent*, July/August 2006

"Brick by Brick," by Manny S., *Represent*, March/April 2008

About
Youth Communication

Youth Communication, founded in 1980, is a nonprofit youth development program located in New York City whose mission is to teach writing, journalism, and leadership skills. The teenagers we train become writers for our websites and books and for two print magazines, *New Youth Connections*, a general-interest youth magazine, and *Represent*, a magazine by and for young people in foster care.

Each year, up to 100 young people participate in Youth Communication's school-year and summer journalism workshops where they work under the direction of full-time professional editors. Most are African American, Latino, or Asian, and many are recent immigrants. The opportunity to reach their peers with accurate portrayals of their lives and important self-help information motivates the young writers to create powerful stories.

Our goal is to run a strong youth development program in which teens produce high quality stories that inform and inspire their peers. Doing so requires us to be sensitive to the complicated lives and emotions of the teen participants while also providing an intellectually rigorous experience. We achieve that goal in the writing/teaching/editing relationship, which is the core of our program.

Our teaching and editorial process begins with discussions

between adult editors and the teen staff. In those meetings, the teens and the editors work together to identify the most important issues in the teens' lives and to figure out how those issues can be turned into stories that will resonate with teen readers.

Once story topics are chosen, students begin the process of crafting their stories. For a personal story, that means revisiting events in one's past to understand their significance for the future. For a commentary, it means developing a logical and persuasive point of view. For a reported story, it means gathering information through research and interviews. Students look inward and outward as they try to make sense of their experiences and the world around them and find the points of intersection between personal and social concerns. That process can take a few weeks or a few months. Stories frequently go through ten or more drafts as students work under the guidance of their editors, the way any professional writer does.

Many of the students who walk through our doors have uneven skills, as a result of poor education, living under extremely stressful conditions, or coming from homes where English is a second language. Yet, to complete their stories, students must successfully perform a wide range of activities, including writing and rewriting, reading, discussion, reflection, research, interviewing, and typing. They must work as members of a team and they must accept individual responsibility. They learn to provide constructive criticism, and to accept it. They engage in explorations of truthfulness, fairness, and accuracy. They meet deadlines. They must develop the audacity to believe that they have something important to say and the humility to recognize that saying it well is not a process of instant gratification. Rather, it usually requires a long, hard struggle through many discussions and much rewriting.

It would be impossible to teach these skills and dispositions as separate, disconnected topics, like grammar, ethics, or assertiveness. However, we find that students make rapid progress when they are learning skills in the context of an inquiry that is personally significant to them and that will benefit their peers.

When teens publish their stories—in *New Youth Connections* and *Represent*, on the web, and in other publications—they reach tens of thousands of teen and adult readers. Teachers, counselors, social workers, and other adults circulate the stories to young people in their classes and out-of-school youth programs. Adults tell us that teens in their programs—including many who are ordinarily resistant to reading—clamor for the stories. Teen readers report that the stories give them information they can't get anywhere else, and inspire them to reflect on their lives and open lines of communication with adults.

Writers usually participate in our program for one semester, though some stay much longer. Years later, many of them report that working here was a turning point in their lives—that it helped them acquire the confidence and skills that they needed for success in college and careers. Scores of our graduates have overcome tremendous obstacles to become journalists, writers, and novelists. They include National Book Award finalist Edwidge Danticat, novelist Ernesto Quinonez, writer Veronica Chambers and *New York Times* reporter Rachel Swarns. Hundreds more are working in law, business, and other careers. Many are teachers, principals, and youth workers, and several have started nonprofit youth programs themselves and work as mentors—helping another generation of young people develop their skills and find their voices.

Youth Communication is a nonprofit educational corporation. Contributions are gratefully accepted and are tax deductible to the fullest extent of the law.

To make a contribution, or for information about our publications and programs, including our catalog of over 100 books and curricula for hard-to-reach teens, see www.youthcomm.org

About The Editors

Laura Longhine is the editorial director at Youth Communication, where she oversees editorial work on the organization's books, websites, and magazines. She edited *Represent*, Youth Communication's magazine by and for teens in foster care, for three years.

Prior to joining Youth Communication, Longhine was a staff writer at the *Free Times*, an alt-weekly in South Carolina, and a freelance reporter for various publications. Her stories have been published in *The New York Times*, *Legal Affairs*, newyorkmetro.com, and *Child Welfare Watch*. She has a bachelor's in English from Tufts University and a master's in journalism from Columbia University.

Longhine is the editor of several other Youth Communication books, including *The Fury Inside: Teens Write About Anger* and *Analyze This! A Teen Guide to Therapy and Getting Help*.

Keith Hefner co-founded Youth Communication in 1980 and has directed it ever since. He is the recipient of the Luther P. Jackson Education Award from the New York Association of Black Journalists and a MacArthur Fellowship. He was also a Revson Fellow at Columbia University.

More Helpful Books
From Youth Comunication

Do You Have What It Takes? A Comprehensive Guide to Success After Foster Care. In this survival manual, current and former foster teens show how they prepared not only for the practical challenges they've faced on the road to independence, but also the emotional ones. Worksheets and exercises help foster teens plan for their future. Activity pages at the end of each chapter help social workers, independent living instructors, and other leaders use the stories with individuals or in groups. (Youth Communication)

The Struggle to Be Strong: True Stories by Teens About Overcoming Tough Times. Foreword by Veronica Chambers. Help young people identify and build on their own strengths with 30 personal stories about resiliency. (Free Spirit)

Depression, Anger, Sadness: Teens Write About Facing Difficult Emotions. Give teens the confidence they need to seek help when they need it. These teens write candidly about difficult emotional problems—such as depression, cutting, and domestic violence—and how they have tried to help themselves. (Youth Communication)

What Staff Need to Know: Teens Write About What Works. How can foster parents, group home staff, caseworkers, social workers, and teachers best help teens? These stories show how communication can be improved on both sides, and provide insight into what kinds of approaches and styles work best. (Youth Communication)

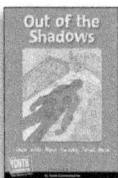

Out of the Shadows: Teens Write About Surviving Sexual Abuse. Help teens feel less alone and more hopeful about overcoming the trauma of sexual abuse. This collection includes first-person accounts by male and female survivors grappling with fear, shame, and guilt. (Youth Communication)

Just the Two of Us: Teens Write About Building Good Relationships. Show teens how to make and maintain healthy relationships (and avoid bad ones). Many teens in care have had poor role models and are emotionally vulnerable. These stories demonstrate good and bad choices teens make in friendship and romance. (Youth Communication)

The Fury Inside: Teens Write About Anger. Help teens manage their anger. These writers show how they got better control of their emotions and sought the support of others. (Youth Communication)

Two Moms in My Heart: Teens Write About the Adoption Option. Teens will appreciate these stories by peers who describe how complicated the adoption experience can be—even when it should give them a more stable home than foster care. (Youth Communication)

My Secret Addiction: Teens Write About Cutting. These true accounts of cutting, or self-mutilation, offer a window into the personal and family situations that lead to this secret habit, and show how teens can get the help they need. (Youth Communication)

Growing Up Together: Teens Write About Being Parents. Give teens a realistic view of the conflicts and burdens of parenthood with these stories from real teen parents. The stories also reveal how teens grew as individuals by struggling to become responsible parents. (Youth Communication)

To order these and other books, go to:
www.youthcomm.org
or call 212-279-0708 x115

www.ingramcontent.com/pod-product-compliance
Lightning Source LLC
Chambersburg PA
CBHW051732090426
42738CB00010B/2221